The Essential Guide for Sort-of Grown Ups

SparkPool

SparkPool

Written by Em Bruce

Designed by Simon Parker
Edited by Alexandra Chapman

Copyright © 2024 Igloo Books Ltd

Published in 2024
First published in the UK by SparkPool Publishing
An imprint of Igloo Books Ltd
Cottage Farm, NN6 0BJ, UK
Owned by Bonnier Books
Sveavägen 56, Stockholm, Sweden

Manufactured in China. 1024 001
10 9 8 7 6 5 4 3 2 1

Library of Congress Cataloging-in-Publication
Data is available upon request.

ISBN 978-1-83795-637-1
igloobooks.com
bonnierbooks.co.uk

Contents

Welcome to Adult Land

ADULTING:

NOUN (N.)

1. When you have a favorite saucepan.

2. When you have to turn the music down in the car in order to see better.

3. The fear of checking your grades becomes the fear of checking your bank account.

Ah, adulthood. As kids, we saw adulthood as the time we'd get a sweet taste of independence; an era of guaranteed fun and boundless freedom that was always just out of reach of our grubby little hands. It was like standing outside the gates of an enchanting theme park of possibility, its bright, twinkling lights taunting us while we were constantly told we'd have to wait in line until we're old enough to visit.

And now you're here! Welcome to Adult Land! The entry fee is kind of steep and, now that you're inside, you're not so sure about some of the rides. There's the Relationship Rollercoaster, the Finance Ferris Wheel, the Careers Carousel and, of course, the Haunted Housework.

Suddenly, you realize you're woefully underprepared for this adventure—but never fear. This book is your personal tour guide to Adult Land, and we're going to show you how to navigate all the rides and make sure you have plenty of fun along the way.

So, if you've just bought yourself this book, congratulations! You've taken the first step to empowering yourself to become the master of Adult Land. (Or maybe this book was a not-so-subtle gift from someone who thinks you're a hot mess. Either way, congrats.)

This book contains all the basic things you need to know how to do but were never taught in school. (You might happen to know how to ask where the swimming pool is in French, but you'd be surprised at how rarely that comes up in job interviews.)

We'll walk you through the ins and outs of some key areas of adulting, including:

- Dating and relationships
- Careers
- Finances
- Household management
- Health and well-being

Remember, it doesn't matter how old you are. Being an "adult" isn't so much a stage of life, it's a state of mind. It's all about embracing your truly independent self, with all the fun, freedom, responsibilities, possibilities, and opportunities that come along with it.

What's in this book?

THE HAUNTED HOUSEWORK

If you're getting too old to call your parents every time you need to change a lightbulb, come face your fears by taking a stroll around the Haunted Housework. In this chapter, you'll learn about all the tricks (and treats) that will help you keep your home running smoothly from top to bottom. From cleaning hacks, moving tips, and decoration inspiration, to how to live with your loved ones in domestic bliss, this is where you'll pick up everything you need to know to become the master of the house.

THE COMMUNITY CREW

As you move from your teenage years into adulthood, the communities you're a part of and your role in them will grow and change significantly. In this section, you'll learn how to find your adult crew, build your connections, and be a valuable member of your various communities. From how to be a good neighbor, a gracious host, and a respectful tourist, to how to use social media to bring about meaningful change in your community, come and discover how you can be a force for good in the world around you.

CHEAT SHEET GOODY BAG

No trip to Adult Land is complete without a goody bag of souvenirs to take home, so don't forget to pick up your cheat sheets at the end of your tour. These are the handy nuggets of knowledge that may have slipped through the cracks but will be worth their weight in gold when life throws you a curveball. From how to craft messages in greeting cards to mastering the art of the apology and harnessing the power of procrastination (yes, you read that right), your Adult Land Cheat Sheet Goody Bag is a treasure trove of bonus tips to help you navigate the rocky road of adulthood.

THE TECH TOWER OF TERROR

As digital natives, we might think we've got tech all wrapped up, but there's no shortage of sudden, gut-wrenching surprises on the Tech Tower of Terror. In this section, you'll learn how to ride the ups and downs of the ever-changing digital landscape, as you harness the power of technology to streamline your life and stay ahead of the curve. From developing good social media habits and curating your digital persona to fighting back against fake news, find out how to navigate the online world like a boss.

KEY SKILLS KIOSK

Swing by the Key Skills Kiosk for quick answers to all those fiddly questions you've been meaning to ask but never have. Like, what do all those symbols on the washing machine mean? Is there a right way to store food in the fridge? How do you actually boil an egg? And then there's the really meaty stuff, like what to do if you lose your passport, how to perform CPR, and what to note if you witness a crime. Let's dive in . . .

THE CAREERS CAROUSEL

Are you looking to kick-start your dream career and climb the ladder of success? Or maybe you haven't quite figured out what you want to do and like the idea of keeping your options open? Wherever you're at in your career journey, this chapter is bursting with handy advice to help set you on the path toward a work life that fulfills your passions, ambitions, and financial goals. Whether you're a side hustler, a nine-to-fiver, or a budding business owner, there's a horse for every rider on the Careers Carousel.

THE FINANCE FERRIS WHEEL

Stop digging down the back of your couch for loose change and get ready to learn how to actually manage your money. In this chapter, you'll unlock the secrets to financial freedom and independence as you learn how to budget like a boss, save like a pro, and invest like a Wall Street wizard. From building an emergency fund to planning for retirement (no, it's not too soon!), you'll pick up all the tips and tricks for taking control of your money and turning your financial dreams into a reality.

THE RELATIONSHIP ROLLERCOASTER

Buckle up as we navigate the heart-stopping twists and turns of adult relationships on the Relationship Rollercoaster. As you get older, your relationships with the most important people in your life will almost inevitably take on new and more complicated dynamics. In this section, we'll equip you with the tools and confidence you need to handle your changing relationships with ease, whether you're dealing with upheavals in your friendship group, dodging generational curses, or dipping your toes into the dating pool.

THE WELL-BEING WALTZERS

In this super-important section, you'll discover how and why to make your health and well-being your top priority as you move into your busy adult life. From chalking up healthy habits to boost your nutrition and perfect your sleep hygiene, to strategies for practicing mindfulness and self-care even when times are tough, you'll empower yourself to nourish your body, mind, and soul and become your own biggest cheerleader on the road to a lifetime of wellness.

Home

AKA THE
HAUNTED
HOUSEWORK

One of the true major milestones of adulthood is moving away from your childhood home and into your own place for the first time. It's the epitome of standing on your own two feet and, for many of us, it's one of the aspects of adult life we look forward to the most. But, as exciting as the promise of independent living might be, it's not all paint swatches and dinner parties.

So, gather round and try not to scream as we begin our tour of Adult Land with a journey through the Haunted Housework. Sure, it looks manageable enough from the outside, but once you move a bit closer, you'll see that each room contains more hurdles than the one before. A sink full of dirty dishes (oh, the *horror*), a hallway table covered in stacks of bills to be paid (make it stop), and a garden full of overgrown weeds that creep over the fence and trigger the goblin who lives next door (quick, turn off the lights so he thinks you're not in!).

Whether you're renting or buying for the first time, you're about to discover that securing and maintaining a home is a lot of day-to-day hard work and responsibility. But don't abandon all hope just yet, because we're going to walk you through every room of the Haunted Housework and give you some simple tips and techniques to tackle everything, from finding and moving into your dream home to cleaning, organizing, and maintaining harmony in your living space. So grab your feather dusters, and let's go to work.

Should you rent or buy?

When it comes to looking for your dream home, you'll either be renting (paying to be a tenant in someone else's property) or buying (owning the property outright). Whether you rent or buy will depend on your personal circumstances, but let's take a look at the pros and cons of both.

PROS AND CONS OF RENTING

PROS	CONS
More flexibility: Need to move for a new job or because your neighbors are a nightmare? So much easier when you're renting.	**Less stability:** Renting isn't permanent, and your landlord could decide to sell the property, start major renovations, or change the rental terms at any time.
Lower upfront costs: Generally, you'll just need the deposit and maybe a month or two of rent upfront, making it more accessible for young adults in particular.	**No equity building:** Unlike monthly mortgage repayments for homeowners, your rent payments don't contribute to you owning the property, so you don't build equity or an asset.
Less responsibility: As a renter, you're typically not responsible for any major repairs or maintenance costs associated with the property. Phew.	**Limited control:** Renters have limited control over the property. You can't do any decorating, renovations, or significant changes without the landlord's approval.
More options: Renting might allow you access to amenities (like an on-site gym or pool) and locations that you might not be able to afford when buying.	**Rental increases:** Your landlord could put the price up every time you renew your lease, making it harder to budget long-term.

WHAT DO YOU NEED BEFORE YOU RENT?

1. DEPOSIT: You'll get this back at the end of the lease term, minus any deductions for damages or unpaid rent.

2. AT LEAST ONE MONTH'S RENT UPFRONT: If there's a lot of competition for a property, offering to pay three or more month's rent upfront may give you the edge.

3. FINANCIAL/INCOME INFORMATION: You may need to provide pay stubs, bank statements, tax returns, or proof of employment to show you can afford to pay the rent.

4. GUARANTOR: You may need to ask someone (usually a family member or close friend) to agree in writing to take responsibility for paying the rent if you can't.

5. PREVIOUS RENTAL HISTORY INFORMATION: This could include references from previous landlords to demonstrate your reliability and suitability.

PROS AND CONS OF BUYING

PROS	CONS
Equity building: As you pay off your mortgage, you build equity in your home, which can increase your net worth over time.	**Financial commitment:** Buying a home requires a significant financial commitment, including upfront and closing costs, and ongoing maintenance expenses.
Stability: Owning a home provides personal and financial stability and lets you build roots, long-term relationships, and routines in your community.	**Less flexibility:** Unlike renting, owning a home ties you to a specific location and property, limiting your ability to adapt to changes in your circumstances.
Freedom to personalize: Unlike renting, owning a home gives you the freedom to personalize and make changes to your home to your heart's content.	**Market fluctuations:** Real estate markets can be unpredictable, and your property value may fluctuate, potentially affecting the value of your investment.
Tax benefits: Homeownership may come with tax benefits, such as deductions for mortgage interest, property taxes, and certain home improvements. Huzzah.	**Risk of foreclosure:** If you can't keep up with mortgage payments, you risk foreclosure, which can have long-term financial consequences and impact on your credit score.

WHAT DO YOU NEED BEFORE YOU BUY?

1. DOWN PAYMENT: A lump sum of money paid upfront toward the purchase price of the property.

2. CLOSING COSTS: Fees associated with finalizing the purchase of the property, including loan origination fees, appraisal fees, title insurance, and legal fees.

3. FINANCIAL DOCUMENTATION: To qualify for a mortgage loan, you'll need to provide proof of income, tax returns, bank statements, and other financial documentation.

4. MORTGAGE PRE-APPROVAL: A letter from a mortgage lender indicating how much you can borrow based on your financial situation and credit rating.

5. APPRAISAL: An assessment of the property's value conducted by a licensed appraiser to ensure the purchase price is in line with market value.

PROPERTY VIEWING CHECKLIST

If you're looking for a property to rent or buy, the first thing to do is to make a list of all your requirements and list them in order of priority. Is it more important that your place is near the train station or that it has outdoor space? Would you rather have off-street parking or a balcony? Then, when you're viewing the property, you essentially want to get as thorough an idea as possible of its condition and your rights and responsibilities as a tenant or owner. Here are a few fundamentals to get your checklist started:

• SECURITY: Check the locks on the doors and windows. Are there any exterior lights?

• NOISE AND LIGHT CONDITIONS: Try to view the property more than once and at different times of the day to get an accurate idea of road noise, neighbor noise, and natural light levels.

• WATER PRESSURE: Run the taps and turn on the shower to see what the water pressure is like (ask first to be polite, but yes, you're allowed to do this!).

• POWER OUTLETS: Where are they and are there enough?

• EXTRACTORS: Are there extractor fans in the kitchen and bathroom?

• MOLD: Are there any signs of mold or water damage?

Moving

So you've found your dream home, good job! The hard part's over, right? Wrong. Now it's time to pack up your life. Moving is consistently listed as one of the most stressful things you can go through, but with a little bit of organization and a whole load of positive mental attitude, it doesn't need to be!

WHAT SHOULD YOU PACK?

It's amazing how much stuff we accumulate, even over a short period of time. Moving is a fantastic opportunity to do a full-life inventory and have a massive clear-out. You only want to pack the essentials, so donate, recycle, or responsibly dispose of the rest. For example, did you know that most saucepans and frying pans have a life expectancy of about five years before the protective coating comes off? This is the perfect opportunity to get rid of some of your shabby bits and invest in upgrades for your new place.

HOW SHOULD YOU PACK?

- Put heavy items (e.g. books) in small boxes.

- In large boxes, spread the heavy items out (e.g. don't have one giant box full of tinned goods, spread them out across a few boxes).

- Use trash bags to pack clothes, bedding, and blankets—this is a great space-saving packing tip and lets you save your boxes for the items that need more protection.

- Label the boxes in as much detail as you have the patience for (you'll thank yourself later).

- Have your essentials box—the things you use every day that you don't pack until the last minute—labeled and easily accessible (clean underwear, charging cables, etc.).

- You might want to give your new place a clean before you unpack, so keep your cleaning products —especially your vacuum cleaner—readily available.

- TOILET PAPER—we cannot stress this enough: keep a stock of toilet paper at hand for your new place. Whether you're moving by yourself or with helpers, at some point, you'll need it and you do not want to be tearing open numerous boxes to find it.

WHEN SHOULD YOU START PACKING?

Right now. No, seriously. Go start packing. You will almost certainly drastically underestimate how long it will take to pack everything up, so start packing *waaaaaaaaay* before you think you need to.

The housemate lottery

If you're moving out of your home and into shared accommodation for the first time, it can be . . . *eye-opening*. Finding good housemates can be a real roll of the dice—even if you're already friends, living together is a whole different story. If you're lucky, you'll feel like you've dropped into an episode of *New Girl*. If not, it might feel more like *The Hunger Games*. Here's how to make sure the odds are ever in your favor when you play the housemate lottery.

TEN TOP TIPS FOR HOUSEMATE HARMONY

1. COMMUNICATE, COMMUNICATE, COMMUNICATE: Open and honest communication is vital. Discuss your expectations, boundaries, and potential issues early on to avoid misunderstandings. You can also schedule regular housemate chats to help keep everyone on the same page.

2. IT'S ALL ABOUT PERSONAL SPACE: Respect your housemates' boundaries, privacy, and belongings to create a harmonious environment.

3. CLEAN UP AFTER YOURSELF: Shared spaces can quickly become messy. Clean up after yourself, whether it's in the kitchen, living room, or bathroom.

4. SHARE THE CHORES: Set up a fair system for chores and responsibilities. Rotating tasks or assigning specific duties can help prevent conflicts over cleanliness.

5. WATCH THE NOISE: Everyone will have different schedules and preferences, so be mindful of noise, especially in the evening and early morning, to maintain a peaceful living environment.

6. HAVE A SYSTEM FOR SHARED EXPENSES: Have open discussions about shared expenses like bills, groceries, and household items to avoid financial conflicts. There are some great (and free) cost-sharing apps for keeping track of all your housemate-y costs.

7. HANDLE CONFLICTS MATURELY: You and your housemates might butt heads from time to time, and that's normal. Address issues calmly and respectfully and be open to compromise.

8. RESPECT EACH OTHER'S DIFFERENCES: Everyone will have different ways of doing things, so be accepting and understanding of differences in habits, culture, and lifestyles.

9. BOND: Make time to socialize with your housemates over shared activities like TV shows, dinners, and outings to build strong, positive housemate relationships.

10. KNOW WHEN TO WALK AWAY: Your home should be a place where you feel relaxed, safe, and supported, so if that's not the case, it might be time to say goodbye. You can make your exit as painless as possible by giving sufficient notice (at least paying up to your notice period if you need to leave sooner), offering to help your housemates find a replacement, and leaving your room and shared spaces nice and clean.

Living with your partner

The recipe for success when living with your partner is pretty similar to living with housemates, but of course, there are some additional unique challenges and things to consider. On top of the tips from the previous page, here are some extra things you might want to keep in mind when building your sweet little love nest.

TIPS FOR DOMESTIC BLISS

1. **HAVE A SYSTEM FOR SHARED EXPENSES:** Okay, so this was already partly covered on the previous page but, with a partner, you may want to consider opening a joint account to handle shared household expenses like bills, rent/mortgage repayments, and food. Make equal contributions (or at least fair contributions you've both agreed on) and ensure you regularly review the balance and discuss any inconsistencies openly and without judgment or accusation.

2. **ENJOY QUALITY TIME TOGETHER OUTSIDE OF THE HOUSE:** When you move in with your partner, you can very easily slip into slightly lazy housebound hang-out habits, such as Netflix binges and takeouts. While these are, of course, perfectly cute and cozy ways to spend time together, make sure that you still make the effort to do fun things outside the house to keep the magic alive.

3. **ENJOY QUALITY TIME APART:** This can be a tricky one to navigate, especially if one of you needs more alone time than the other, but make sure you give your partner plenty of space and be considerate of their boundaries. Have an open and honest conversation about this and make an effort to learn your partner's rhythms and anticipate when they might need a bit of room.

4. **(RE)LEARN EACH OTHER'S BOUNDARIES:** Skip ahead to page 100 to learn all about how setting and respecting each other's boundaries is the key to creating a healthy relationship based on trust and respect. If you've already had this conversation with your partner earlier in the relationship (10 points to you), you may need to revisit this once you've moved in together to see if your boundaries are slightly different now that you're living in such close quarters.

5. **PRACTICE PATIENCE AND EMPATHY:** This is even more important than when living with housemates because—perhaps for the first time—when you move in with your partner, you're going to see each other warts and all. Whether that's getting an insight into their bathroom habits (the ultimate love test), taking care of them when they're sick, or comforting them after a bad day at work, you'll need to utilize all the patience and understanding you've got to take the rough with the smooth and let this new chapter of your relationship unfold authentically.

To DIY or not to DIY, that is the question

At some point (usually the most inconvenient), something in your home is going to stop working, and you'll be faced with the question, "Can I fix this myself?". Whether you fancy yourself as a bit of a DIY master or you get nervous about changing the batteries in the TV remote, it's important to know what you can try your hand at and when you should call in the pros.

DO IT YOURSELF

Here's a list of everyday tasks that you may be able to handle yourself. If you have limitations with mobility or you feel unsure about how to safely do any of these, it's always better to ask for help. Even getting someone (or a YouTube tutorial) to show you how to do it for the first time can give you the confidence you need to tackle it by yourself in the future.

EVERYONE:

* changing lightbulbs
* assembling flatpack furniture
* fixing loose doorknobs, hinges, or screws
* fixing squeaky doors
* basic garden care (e.g., de-weeding, cutting the grass).

HOMEOWNERS ONLY:

* painting
* installing shelves
* hanging paintings, pictures, or mirrors
* installing curtain rods or blinds
* patching holes in the walls.

DON'T DO IT YOURSELF:

* gas work
* electrical work
* fixing faulty fire alarms (seriously, don't mess with them)
* plumbing repairs beyond basic attempts to unclog a drain (see page 165 for tips)
* roof repairs
* structural work
* removing asbestos
* tackling a pest infestation
* repairing mold damage
* installing, repairing or maintaining HVAC (heating, ventilation, air conditioning) systems.

If in doubt, check online and ask for help. Many repair or maintenance companies will be happy to offer you advice or a quote at no charge. You should never feel embarrassed to ask for help: it's a great way to learn and build your adult life skills (and it's far more embarrassing to have to explain why the contents of your toilet is dripping down the stairs).

Home insurance

DO YOU NEED HOME INSURANCE?

If insurance is one of those adult-y words that you hear a lot but never really know what people are talking about, don't worry—we've got you covered. Here's a run-through of the what, the why, and the how of home insurance to help you make an informed decision.

WHAT IS HOME INSURANCE?

Home insurance is kind of like a monthly subscription. You pay a certain amount of money each month to your insurance provider and if something happens to your home—like getting damaged in a fire or someone breaking in and stealing your stuff—your insurance provider helps you cover the costs to fix or replace things. It's basically like having a backup plan in case something bad happens to your home.

WHY GET HOME INSURANCE?

1. FINANCIAL PROTECTION: Home insurance can cover (in whole or in part) the cost of repairs or replacements that you might need in case of unexpected events, such as theft, fire, or natural disasters.

2. LIABILITY PROTECTION: Home insurance also provides you with liability protection in case someone is injured on your property or if you accidentally damage someone else's property. This can help protect you from costly legal expenses.

3. PEACE OF MIND: Having home insurance might help you sleep a little easier at night knowing that your home and valuables are protected against any unexpected plot twists.

HOW TO CHOOSE HOME INSURANCE

1. SHOP AROUND: Take the time to research and compare quotes from different insurance providers to find the best coverage for you at the best price. Make sure you carefully review and understand the coverage provided by different policies and pay attention to things like coverage limits, deductibles, exclusions, and optional add-ons to ensure you've got the right level of protection for your needs.

2. READ REVIEWS: Make sure you check out the customer reviews for the insurance provider you're considering to get an insight into people's real-life experiences with the company. Take note of things like customer service, how quickly claims were processed, and whether the company was reliable and honest in their dealings.

3. CUSTOMIZE YOUR COVERAGE: Home insurance policies typically include coverage for personal belongings such as furniture, electronics, jewelry, and other valuables, but many policies also offer customizable coverage options so you can tailor your policy to suit your individual needs and budget. So, if you have valuable items such as gadgets, art, or collectables, you can choose additional coverage for them to ensure they're adequately protected.

Home is not a place— it's a feeling.

Putting your stamp on your home

Now you're all moved in, it's time to make the place your own. Depending on whether you're sharing with someone else or you've got the place all to yourself (and, of course, whether you've bought or rented), you'll have varying amounts of control over how much personalizing you can do, but here are some good general rules to follow to make your house a home.

HOW TO OPTIMIZE YOUR SPACE

- GET THE LIGHTING RIGHT: Make the most of your natural light (a well-placed mirror or two can work magic on amplifying natural light). If your place doesn't get much natural light, invest in some lamps or strip lights to attach to things like bookcases and shelves (but only if they belong to you!). Even simple changes like swapping out light bulbs for ones with a higher wattage can make a huge difference.

- HAVE A NEUTRAL BASE: As a general rule, it's best to keep the walls and carpet a light, neutral color and add your pops of color, texture, and character with things like cushions, rugs, and curtains. If you change your style, it's a lot easier to swap out soft furnishings than to recarpet, repaint, or replace the wallpaper.

- ADD SOME PERSONAL TOUCHES: Depending on the rules for your place, hanging artwork and pictures (if you're renting, you may be able to use removable hooks—check first!) or displaying pictures on surfaces along with your other décor pieces can really make it feel like home.

- DON'T FORGET THE GREENERY: A little splash of greenery goes a long way by breathing life into your home. Head to page 28 to learn how to be a plant parent (and if you're an incurable plant murderer, some good-quality fake foliage should do the trick without adding to your body count).

- TAKE IT SLOW: As much as you might want to get your new place looking exactly like the Pinterest board you made before the movers had even reached the end of the driveway, don't rush into it. Remember, less is more, so just start with the essentials, live in the space for a while, and let the finishing touches evolve naturally.

- KEEP YOUR HOME CLUTTER-FREE: Let the size of your space determine how much stuff you have, not the other way around. This means if your wardrobe is bursting at the seams, don't buy a bigger closet; donate some of your clothes! Also, allocate a drawer as "the junk drawer"—this may seem counterintuitive, but you'll always know where to look for some of your random items, like hair ties, loose batteries, and pens.

How to organize your wardrobe

If it takes you ages to get ready because; a) you can never find what you're looking for; b) you don't know what half the things in your closet are or; c) your closet is bursting with clothes and accessories for the wrong season, it might be time to reorganize. Follow these simple tips to help you make the most of your space, stay organized, and ensure that you always have the perfect outfit on hand for any occasion.

1. MAXIMIZE YOUR SPACE: When it comes to organizing your closet, it's all about making the most of the space you have. Stock up on space-saving storage solutions like hanging organizers and stackable or under-bed storage boxes to make use of every nook and cranny of available space. You can even flex your DIY muscles by adding shelves or hooks for additional storage (but remember to double-check first if you're renting).

2. GET ORGANIZED: Once you've got all your storage solutions in place, it's time to tackle the daunting task of organizing your clothing. Chuck your favorite playlist on and start by sorting your items into categories—tops, bottoms, workwear, gym clothes, underwear, etc. Then, within each category, organize your clothing by color, style, or season to make it easier to grab what you need during those uh-oh-I-slept-in mornings.

3. CONSIDER A CAPSULE WARDROBE: If you're all about living that minimal life and hate having to decide what to wear every morning, why not embrace the capsule wardrobe? A capsule wardrobe is essentially a carefully curated collection of a few versatile, high-quality pieces that you can mix and match to make effortlessly stylish combinations. Invest in some classic staples in neutral, timeless colors to save yourself time, effort, space, and money, and become a beacon of sustainable style.

4. DO A SEASONAL SWAP: As the seasons change, so too will your closet. To make the seasonal swap a breeze, designate specific times of the year to rotate your clothing. At the end of each season, pack away out-of-season items in storage boxes or vacuum-sealed bags to free up space for the things you'll actually be wearing this season. Plus, the added bonus is that you'll kind of forget about the things you store, so when you're ready to wear them again, it's like getting a whole new closet!

5. DECLUTTER: The seasonal swap is also a fantastic opportunity to review your closet and pick out a few items that can be donated or sold. Are you putting clothes into storage that you didn't wear once this season? It might be time to give them a new home with someone who will get the most out of them. Or, if they're in good condition, you could even sell them and use the money to buy yourself something you'll actually wear!

Working-from-home hacks

Remote working is now more popular than ever and, as you take your first steps into the world of work, you might have the option to double-up your home as your place of work. On paper, working from home feels like such a dream: rolling out of bed and being in the "office" 30 seconds later without having to battle through rain, traffic, and grumpy commuters. That is, until the cat knocks your coffee all over your laptop, your neighbor decides to whip out their leaf blower during your virtual meeting (again), and you spend your evenings answering emails and finishing off "just one more" task. But, by following these simple steps, you can set yourself up for a healthy work-life balance and optimize your productivity and mental clarity when working from home.

YOUR WFH CHECKLIST

1. Comfortable, ergonomic chair.

2. Laptop/screen at the right height.

3. Plenty of natural light, where possible.

4. If you can't sit by a window, make sure you have a lamp.

5. Don't work where you sleep/eat/relax. If possible, have a designated working space, as this will help your brain compartmentalize your work life and your non-work life.

HOW TO WORK FROM HOME EFFECTIVELY

- TIP 1: Set yourself an alarm or use a habits app to remind you to stand up and move around for at least 5 –10 minutes every hour.

- TIP 2: Get into a routine. Set yourself a start and finish time for your work day and stick to them (as much as possible).

- TIP 3: Get dressed for work. As tempting as it might be to work in your PJs, dressing up in smart-casual clothing will get you into the right mindset to work.

- TIP 4: Take regular screen breaks. Use the 20/20 rule and spend 20 seconds looking away from your screen every 20 minutes.

- TIP 5: Interact with others (no, this doesn't include the dog). It's super important to maintain your social bonds when working from home. Consider trying out a co-working space one day a week or working from a café to avoid feeling isolated.

Clean and green

When you head to the household cleaning section of the supermarket, you'll be bombarded with a kaleidoscope of colorful, chemical-crammed cleaning products. Not only are these products often super expensive, they're almost always terrible for the environment. Enter: the homemade cleaning product craze. Making your own cleaning products is easy, cheap, and *way* better for the planet. What are you waiting for?

WHAT YOU'LL NEED

- Reusable bottles (including spray bottles)
- Water
- White vinegar
- Lemon juice
- Baking soda
- Essential oils (tea tree and peppermint are particularly useful)*
- Hydrogen peroxide*
- Liquid dish soap

CLEANING PRODUCT	WATER	VINEGAR	BAKING SODA	LEMON JUICE	ESSENTIAL OIL	LIQUID DISH SOAP	HYDROGEN PEROXIDE	METHOD
All-purpose cleaner	1 cup	1 cup	1 tbsp		10 drops (optional)			Combine into a spray bottle and shake to mix.
Glass cleaner	1 cup	1 cup		1 tbsp				Combine into a spray bottle and shake to mix.
Drain unblocker	5 cups (hot)	1 cup	1 cup					Pour baking soda down the drain followed by vinegar. Leave for 30 mins, then pour in hot water.
Floor cleaner	16 cups (warm)	1 cup				1 tbsp		Combine into a spray bottle or bucket and mix well.
Mold and mildew remover	1 cup	1 cup			1 tsp tea tree			Combine into a spray bottle. Apply to the affected area, let it sit for an hour and then scrub.
Rust remover			Enough to make a paste	1/2 cup				Mix to form a paste. Let it sit on the affected area for a few hours then scrub.
Limescale remover		1 cup	Enough to cover area	1 tbsp				Sprinkle baking soda onto the affected area, then spray with the vinegar/lemon solution.
Grout cleaner			1/2 cup			1 tsp	1/4 cup	Mix to form a paste. Let it sit on the affected area for 15 minutes then scrub.

*Please follow safety instructions for the individual products you use for these recipes and ensure the finished cleaning products are always kept out of the reach of children.

How to *actually* clean the house

So you've got all your homemade green cleaning supplies—where do you begin? Snap on those rubber gloves as we go top to bottom to find out how to *actually* clean your house.

THE BASICS IN FIVE STEPS

1. TIDY FIRST, THEN CLEAN: Put things away and clear the surfaces as much as possible before you start cleaning.

2. DO THE WET AREAS FIRST: This means the kitchen and bathroom. These tend to need the most work, so you should get them out of the way before your get-up-and-go has got-up-and-gone.

3. START AT THE TOP: Next up, you want to dust and clean everything up high—ceilings, fans, light fixtures, and the tops of shelves and cupboards. This way, all the dust and dirt falls downward onto the yet-to-be-cleaned surfaces.

4. WORK YOUR WAY DOWN: Move down, dusting and wiping the mid-level surfaces like tables, chairs, and desks.

5. DO THE FLOORS: Finally, vacuum everywhere thoroughly and mop the floors last.

Daily:

- Make your bed (do it, you'll feel amazing).
- Wipe down surfaces, especially in the kitchen and bathroom.
- Clean the dishes.
- Put your clothes away.
- Tidy away any clutter.

Weekly:

- Wash your sheets, pillowcases, and comforter.
- Wash fabrics like towels, bath mats, rugs, cushion covers, and blankets.
- Clean the toilet, bath and/or shower, and sinks.
- Wipe down the inside of the oven and microwave.
- Wash the windows and mirrors.
- Dust all surfaces.
- Vacuum and mop the floors.

Monthly:

- Scrub grout.
- Dust/wipe down the baseboards.
- Wipe inside all cupboards.
- Clear any expired food out of the fridge.
- Dust/wipe around the windows and doors.
- Wipe down the inside of the trash bin.
- Flush the drains with your homemade clean green drain unblocker (see page 21).

How to be responsible for your waste

Making a positive impact on the environment isn't all about grand gestures or drastic lifestyle changes. Sometimes, it's the small, everyday actions that add up to make a big difference. From embracing the joys of second-hand shopping to mastering the art of responsible waste disposal, here are a few simple tips to help you minimize your environmental impact and help build a healthier, more sustainable planet for our future.

SUSTAINABILITY FIRST

- BE A THRIFTY SHOPPER: Instead of constantly feeding into the cycle of fast fashion, consider shopping second-hand for clothing, furniture, and household items. Not only does this help reduce the demand for new products, but it also gives pre-loved items a new lease of life and prevents them from ending up in landfills (plus, you'll score some cute, unique pieces that will be the envy of all who lay eyes on them).

- REPAIR IT TO SPARE IT: If something gets broken, damaged, or stained, try to fix it yourself and extend its life rather than just throwing it away. There's almost nothing you can't learn from a YouTube tutorial, so roll up your sleeves and repair it to spare it from landfill.

- RECYCLE RESPONSIBLY: While recycling is important, it's equally important to do it right. Familiarize yourself with your local recycling guidelines and make sure to clean and sort your recyclables properly. And remember, not everything can be recycled—items like plastic bags, Styrofoam™, and dirty or food-contaminated materials may need to be thrown out instead.

- TOP TIP: Avoid the temptation to throw things in the recycling if you're not 100% sure they can be recycled—this can contaminate the whole bin and everything might end up in landfill (which pretty much defeats the whole purpose).

Supermarkets and general stores often have trash bins where you can drop off your used batteries and lightbulbs (which generally can't go in the regular trash).

Spring cleaning for every season

Despite what the name might suggest, spring cleans aren't just for spring. They're a great all-year-round opportunity to improve your mental clarity, boost your productivity, or welcome in a new chapter of your life by blowing away the spiderwebs.

IS IT A GOOD TIME FOR A SPRING CLEAN?

Of course it is! Any time is a good time for a spring clean, but here are some particularly good opportunities to spring clean your life:

- when you start a new job
- after a breakup
- before you move house
- before you redecorate
- the start of a new season
- the start of a new year.

SPRING CLEAN CLEAR-OUT CHECKLIST

Before the big clean comes the big clear-out! Depending on how frequently you declutter, you might have a lot or a little to throw out, but the more you do it, the easier it will become. Do some research to find out how you can responsibly dispose of these common clutter-creators in your local area.

ITEM	SELL	DONATE	RECYCLE	THROW
Shoes and clothes in good condition				
Shoes and clothing in unusable condition				
Bedding in good condition				
Bedding in unusable condition				
Pillows and comforters (not covers)				
Old magazines, newspapers, and pens				
Expired food				
Broken electronics				
Books, games, and puzzles				
Unused or expired medication				
Old greetings cards				
Used batteries				
Old paperwork				

Are you a minimalist or a magpie?

If you collect knick-knacks like a squirrel collects nuts, you probably own things you absolutely don't need. Take the quiz to find out if you're on top of your clutter or if your clutter is getting on top of you. Check mark each statement that applies to you, then count them up to find out how you score!

1. You have loose batteries lying around that are definitely dead.
2. You could build a three-story house with your Tupperware™ collection.
3. You still have CDs and/or VHS tapes—but no CD or VHS players.
4. You have old birthday cards from years ago.
5. You have a box of keepsakes from an ex.
6. You still have your old textbooks from school/university.
7. You have a dozen fancy notebooks that you've never written in.
8. You always accept freebies even if you don't want or need them.
9. You have expired medicine in the bathroom.
10. You have a drawer full of mystery cables and chargers.
11. You have a pile of old movie/festival/gig/plane tickets.
12. You have a collection of odd socks that would make a house-elf's Christmas.
13. You have a drawer full of takeout menus even though you always order online.
14. You have no fewer than three novelty keyrings on your keys.
15. You have books on your shelf that you're never going to read again.
16. You have at least one appliance that's broken beyond repair.
17. You have clothes that you haven't worn in five years.
18. You have unopened mail that you received over a month ago.
19. You have a large collection of miniature or sample beauty products.
20. You have stuff stored somewhere other than your home.

0–5 POINTS = MINIMALISM MASTER
Congratulations! You've mastered the art of minimalism. Your living space is organized, clutter-free, and tidy.

6–10 POINTS = CASUAL COLLECTOR
You might have a few areas that could use some tidying up, but on the whole, you're keeping your clutter collection to a minimum. Good job!

11–15 POINTS = TIPPING POINT
If you're struggling to find things amidst the mess, it might be time to do some clutter crowd control before things get out of hand.

16–20 POINTS = HOARDING HORROR
Consider this your intervention. It's time to get ruthless and sacrifice some stuff for a more comfortable living space. You can do it!

Make your home your haven

Whether you're a self-proclaimed design aficionado or just looking to spruce up your space, the popular interior design principles of feng shui, hygge, and wabi-sabi might just hold the key to transforming your home into a haven of comfort and balance that best reflects your personality. So, grab your favorite throw blanket, light some candles, and get ready to discover your next interior design obsession.

GETTING INTO THE FLOW WITH FENG SHUI

Imagine your home as a giant game of Tetris™, where every piece slots perfectly into place to create a harmonious flow of energy. That's the essence of feng shui! This ancient Chinese practice focuses on arranging furniture, colors, and décor to promote positive energy and harmony in your living space. From decluttering your entryway to incorporating elements of nature like plants and water features, feng shui teaches us that a well-balanced home leads to a well-balanced life (makes sense, right?). So, why not try your hand at this ancient art and feng shui your way to a home full of good vibes.

HOME IS WHERE THE HYGGE IS

Ever wondered why Danish people are always at the top of those lists of the happiest folks on the planet? The answer might be hygge! Pronounced "hoo-gah," this Danish concept is all about embracing coziness, warmth, and an all-over feeling of contentment in your living space. Picture curling up with a good book and a cup of hot cocoa by the fireplace, surrounded by soft blankets and flickering candles—you're picturing hygge! So, dim the lights, break out the fuzzy socks, and create a cozy sanctuary where you can escape the stresses of the outside world and turn your home into a cave of hygge-inspired comfort.

EMBRACING IMPERFECTION WITH WABI-SABI

In a world obsessed with filtered perfection, wabi-sabi is here to remind us that true beauty lies in imperfect authenticity. Hailing from Japan, this philosophy celebrates the natural flaws and quirks that make each object and space unique. From handmade pottery with visible cracks to weathered wooden furniture that tells a story, wabi-sabi encourages us to embrace the beauty of impermanence and find joy in life's fleeting moments. So, next time someone points out your chipped mug or that slightly crooked picture frame—just tell them you're adding a touch of wabi-sabi charm to your home, *thank you very much.*

"The best way to find out what we really need is to get rid of what we don't."

MARIE KONDO

How to be a good plant parent

Adding plants to your home is a fantastic way to breathe some life and natural beauty into your space while boosting your health and well-being. From purifying the air to reducing stress and boosting creativity, there's no end to the benefits of surrounding yourself with these leafy beauties.

PLANT PARENTING ESSENTIALS

- **CHOOSE CAREFULLY:** When picking your plants, it's better to start small and build your confidence as a plant parent than to dive in headfirst and risk overwhelming yourself (and your plants). Start by selecting low-maintenance varieties that require minimal attention.

- **LIGHT IT UP:** Before you bring your new leafy friend home, take note of the lighting conditions in your space and choose plants that are compatible with your home's natural light levels. If you notice your plants leaning toward light sources, make sure you rotate them regularly to stop them from growing lopsided and toppling over.

- **WATER WISELY:** Did you know that overwatering is one of the most common pitfalls for new plant parents? Instead of sticking to a rigid watering schedule, get to know your plants and their individual needs. Check the soil's moisture regularly by sticking your finger in the soil and only water when the top few centimeters feel dry to the touch.

- **GIVE THEM SPACE:** Again, just like people, plants need room to grow and spread their roots. If you notice your plant's growth starting to slow down or the soil drying out more quickly than usual, it might be time to move it into a bigger pot.

- **SHOW THEM SOME LOVE:** Last but certainly not least, being a good plant parent is about giving your plants plenty of love and attention.

TOP 10 POPULAR HOUSEPLANTS	LOW LIGHT	LOW MAINTENANCE	PET FRIENDLY
Fiddle-leaf fig	✗	✗	✗
Monstera	✗	✓	✗
Rubber plant	✗	✓	✗
ZZ plant	✓	✓	✗
Spider plant	✓	✓	✓
Snake plant	✓	✓	✗
Philodendron	✓	✓	✗
Pothos	✓	✓	✗
Cast iron plant	✓	✓	✓
Peace lily	✓	✓	✗

Should you get a pet?

Whether you grew up surrounded by animals or in a strict no-pet household, with adulthood comes the power to become the pet parent you've always dreamed of. But, with great power comes great responsibility so, before you dive headfirst into the world of wagging tails and whiskery kisses, it's important to think very carefully about how a furry, feathered, or scaly friend will fit into your lifestyle.

THE PROS AND CONS OF PET PARENTHOOD

PROS: On the one paw, having a pet can bring boundless joy, companionship, and unconditional love into your life. From endless cuddles to hilarious antics, pets have a magical way of brightening even the darkest of days. Plus, studies have shown that living with a pet can have numerous physical and mental health benefits, including reduced stress, lower blood pressure, and increased exercise levels (for example, taking your dog on a daily walk or chasing your cat around the house because it's stolen your sock).

CONS: Pet ownership also comes with its fair share of responsibilities and challenges. You've got to factor in the significant costs of food, insurance, vet bills, and upkeep as well as the time and energy it takes to train, socialize, and shower your pet with all the day-to-day attention and stimulation it needs to thrive. Still sure you want a pet? Read on to narrow down your pawfect pairing.

DIFFERENT PET NEEDS

- Dogs are incredibly loving and rewarding pets, but possibly the most high-maintenance option. Every dog is different but, in general, they need a hefty daily dose of exercise, mental stimulation, and social interaction, so don't even think about becoming a dog owner unless you can dedicate serious time and energy to your canine companion. If you're out of the house all day, you may also need to pay for a dog walking service or doggy daycare, which can be pretty pricey over a dog's lifetime (around 10–13 years).

- Cats are more independent by nature but still require mental and physical stimulation to stay happy and healthy. You'll need to provide them with plenty of toys, scratching posts, and climbing structures along with daily interactive play sessions to keep them engaged and entertained (and not tearing up your curtains). Cats are generally fine being left to their own devices during the day, so they might be a better option if you're out of the house a lot.

- Although slightly lower-maintenance options, smaller furries (e.g., rabbits, guinea pigs, and hamsters), reptiles, and birds still need appropriate housing, food, exercise, and mental stimulation. Research your chosen species thoroughly to understand how you can make sure your pet lives a long and happy life.

Some types of pets may be prohibited in your area due to local laws, so make sure you read up on this first and follow the rules for responsible pet ownership. Finally, adopt, don't shop! Whatever kind of pet you've got your heart set on, consider adopting or rehoming one from a reputable rescue center or charity and give a loving home to an animal that needs it most.

Careers

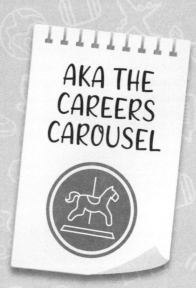

AKA THE
CAREERS
CAROUSEL

Gather round, gather round, and feast your eyes on the Careers Carousel! Just like the brightly colored horses moving up and down on the carousel, each with their own unique style and charm, careers come in all shapes and sizes, and finding the perfect steed for your journey into the world of work can sometimes seem like an impossible task.

From traditional nine-to-five jobs to freelance gigs and side hustles, the Careers Carousel has something for everyone. But wait, we didn't even tell you the best news yet! At any time, you're allowed to stop the ride and swap to another horse—or just take a break from the Careers Carousel altogether!

That's right, as you move into the world of work, you can feel somewhat reassured that the routes into employment are diverse, flexible, and very rarely perfectly linear, and that with a sprinkle of determination and perseverance, you can navigate the ups and downs of the job market gracefully with the wind in your hair.

In this chapter, we'll take a spin around the Careers Carousel together, exploring the various career options available to you and providing practical advice for finding your place in the professional world. Whether you're a recent graduate just starting out or a seasoned professional looking for a change, the Careers Carousel promises to be an exhilarating ride filled with discovery and opportunity. So, pick a horse (it doesn't matter which one), grab hold of the reins, and get ready to ride your way to the career of your dreams!

Picking your career path

When you were a kid, you probably had a ready-made answer to the question, "What do you want to be when you grow up?". An astronaut, a mermaid, a knight, a superhero, a kitten? All excellent options. But as you enter the rocky territory of adulthood, you may find that your ambitions have changed somewhat, and narrowing your passions and skills into a career path isn't quite so straightforward. If you're still figuring it all out, here's how to steer yourself in the right direction (or maybe you already know exactly what you want to do and are well on your way to smashing your career goals, in which case, you can skip this part and go make a snack instead).

QUESTIONS TO ASK YOURSELF

The first and most important step on your career journey is spending lots of time reflecting on what makes you tick. Having a clear understanding of your skills, interests, and ambitions is how you unlock shortcuts to get to the center of the career maze (instead of just wandering around aimlessly hoping you don't get eaten by the Minotaur).

- What are my interests?
- What am I good at?
- Who do I want to work with (adults, kids, animals, the general public)?
- Where do I want to work (from home, in an office, outdoors, overseas, in a big city)?
- What are my financial goals?
- Do I want to continue my studies?

HOW TO NARROW IT DOWN

- TRY EVERYTHING: Volunteer work, internships, and part-time jobs are a great way to dip your toes into different industries and roles and gain some valuable hands-on experience at the same time.
- GET QUIZZICAL: Take as many online quizzes and career assessments as you can to see what ideas they give out that might align with your skills and interests.
- NETWORK LIKE A PRO: Connect with professionals in your field(s) of interest, attend career fairs and events, and build your personal brand online. You never know when a chance encounter or a well-timed LinkedIn message could lead to your dream job!
- KEEP AN OPEN MIND: Career success stories are full of people who stumbled into their dream job due to an unexpected twist of fate or because the job they hoped for fell through. Keep your options open and look out for hidden gems and opportunities that may not be obvious at first glance.

Résumé tips and tricks

Your résumé (also known as a CV) is one of the trickiest and most important documents you'll ever create. Most of the time, it will be the first impression an employer gets of you, and it could make or break whether you get invited for that coveted first interview. Here's how to make sure your résumé stands out from the crowd and gives you the best chance of getting your foot in the door.

TIP: Use a professional yet engaging tone, providing context and storytelling to bring your experiences to life.
TRICK: Use active voice ("I achieved this by . . .") instead of passive voice ("This was achieved by . . ."). Bring receipts (numbers, percentages, or concrete examples) to quantify your achievements whenever possible.

TIP: Avoid unnecessary details or wordiness.
TRICK: Trim down repeated or excessive information that doesn't add value or directly contribute to your candidacy (it's wonderful that you were the undefeated potato-sack-race champion at your school, but it's probably time to remove it from your résumé).

TIP: Triple-check for spelling and grammar errors, as well as formatting inconsistencies.
TRICK: Ask a friend, family member, or mentor to review your résumé with fresh eyes—a second pair of eyes can catch mistakes you might have missed.

TIP: Keep it concise and focused—aim for one page if possible (two pages max).
TRICK: Use bullet points to highlight key achievements and responsibilities. Prioritize relevance and impact—include experiences and skills that align with your career goals and demonstrate your value to potential employers.

TIP: Be honest and transparent, representing yourself accurately and authentically.
TRICK: Avoid exaggerating or embellishing your experiences—honesty is key to building trust with potential employers and lying really isn't worth it!

TIP: Treat your résumé as a living document, updating it regularly with new skills, experiences, and accomplishments—even when you're not actively job-hunting.
TRICK: Set yourself a regular reminder (maybe once or twice a year) to spend a few hours updating and sprucing up your résumé (bonus tip: you can make this more fun and productive by doing it with a friend!).

TIP: Include a skills section early on, listing the relevant technical and soft skills that are valuable to your target industry.
TRICK: Tailor your skills to the job description, emphasizing those that are most sought after by employers in your field.

TIP: Opt for a clean and visually appealing layout—you're aiming for readability and professionalism.
TRICK: Use consistent formatting, fonts, and spacing, and avoid overly decorative elements that may distract from the content.

Nailing the interview

You did it! You polished your résumé to perfection and got invited for an in-person (or virtual) interview —congratulations! But then . . . the fear sets in. *What questions might they ask? What if I don't have an answer? What should I wear?* Take a deep breath. With the right preparation and mindset, you can ace your interview and make a lasting impression on your prospective employer.

BEFORE THE INTERVIEW

- **RESEARCH, RESEARCH, RESEARCH:** Thoroughly research the company, its culture, values, and industry trends before the interview. If the salary is not specified, research salary ranges for similar positions and come up with a broad range you'd be ready to accept.

- **PREPARE:** Using the job description as your starting point, jot down as many questions as you can possibly imagine that the interviewer might ask. Prepare and memorize answers for each one, making sure they fit your specific skills and experience to the role and the company's mission and goals.

- **PRACTICE:** Ask a friend or family member to practice interviewing you. Get them to throw you curveballs so you can get comfortable thinking on your feet.

DURING THE INTERVIEW

- **DRESS FOR SUCCESS:** Take cues from the company's dress code and culture (see if you can find pics online) and choose an outfit that makes you feel confident and comfortable and allows your personality to shine through while still presenting a polished image.

- **DON'T PANIC:** If you get asked a question you don't have an answer to, have some honest, professional responses up your sleeve, such as, "That's not an area I currently have much experience in, but I'd love the chance to learn more about it" or, "I'm afraid I don't have that information at hand, but I'd be more than happy to follow up with you after the interview."

- **BACK YOURSELF:** If the interviewer asks for your salary expectations (cue sweaty palms), offer the range you've come up with, explain that it's based on your research, experience, and the value you bring to the role and emphasize your willingness to negotiate.

- **"DO YOU HAVE ANY QUESTIONS FOR US?":** Have a few insightful questions prepared to ask the interviewer (remember, the interview is also for *you* to decide if you want to work for *them*).

AFTER THE INTERVIEW

- **FOLLOW UP:** Send a personalized thank-you email or note within 24 hours of the interview. Express gratitude for the interviewer's time and the opportunity to interview and reiterate your interest in the job.

Dealing with problematic personalities in the workplace

So you've got the job (obviously, because you're amazing) and it's all going great . . . until you come across a problematic personality. This, unfortunately, is a fact of life in the workplace, whether it's a difficult customer, client, or colleague. The tricky part is that you can't exactly ignore them, so how can you go about creating a harmonious relationship with these complex people?

- SPOT THE SIGNS: Problematic personalities in the workplace might not always be immediately evident. Keep an eye out for the more subtle signs, such as people who are lazy, push your boundaries, cause distractions, or try to entangle you in gossip or drama.

- KEEP YOUR COOL: Maintain professionalism at all times. By remaining calm, composed, and focused on the task at hand, you can avoid getting drawn into confrontation or emotional outbursts that escalate tensions, hinder productivity, and jeopardize your own reputation.

- PUT YOURSELF IN THEIR SHOES: Summon up all your empathy and try to understand the other person's perspective. We never really know what people are going through behind the scenes, so try to establish common ground and find a way to work together.

- SET BOUNDARIES: Establish clear boundaries to protect your well-being and maintain a healthy work environment. Communicate assertively and respectfully when your boundaries are crossed, and be prepared to enforce consequences if necessary.

- FOCUS ON SOLUTIONS: Instead of dwelling on the problem, shift your focus to identifying practical solutions and taking proactive steps to address the issues. Just this shift in mindset can go a long way to make you feel more hopeful about the situation.

- SEEK SUPPORT: If someone's behavior makes you feel uncomfortable, unsafe, or unable to do your job properly, it's time to communicate with higher-ups. Speak to your mentor, boss, or HR department and explain any methods or steps you've already taken to try to resolve the matter on your own.

- LOOK AFTER YOURSELF: If you're having to deal with difficult people on a regular basis, make self-care a priority so that you have the physical and emotional energy required to maintain your composure and calm demeanor. Take time to recharge and rejuvenate through activities such as mindfulness, exercise, and hobbies that bring you joy and relaxation.

- LOOK AT IT AS A LEARNING OPPORTUNITY: As unpleasant as they may be, every interaction with a difficult person is an opportunity for growth and development. Reflect on the lessons you've learned through challenging situations and use them to improve your interpersonal skills, grit, and emotional intelligence. By embracing these learning opportunities, you'll emerge stronger, more resilient, and more empathetic than ever.

Recognizing and responding to toxic behavior in the workplace

As you discovered on the previous page, the workplace can be full of challenging personalities, but there's a difference between tricky people and bullies. It's super important to be able to spot the signs of workplace bullying—both when it's directed at you and other people—and know what steps to take when you detect it.

WHAT IS WORKPLACE BULLYING?

Workplace bullying encompasses a range of toxic behaviors, from overt acts of aggression to subtle forms of manipulation and intimidation. It can manifest in various ways, such as verbal abuse, harassment, exclusion, sabotage, or the misuse of power and authority to undermine others. Recognizing these behaviors is the first step in addressing workplace bullying effectively.

HOW TO SPOT THE SIGNS OF BULLYING

If you find yourself (or another person) being consistently belittled, singled out, or ridiculed by a colleague or superior, this is workplace bullying in action. Common signs of bullying include being subjected to unfair criticism, having your work sabotaged or undermined, being excluded from meetings or social events, or experiencing verbal abuse or intimidation.

WHAT TO DO IF YOU OR SOMEONE ELSE IS BEING BULLIED

Addressing workplace bullying is an extremely brave thing to do. It requires courage, assertiveness, and a commitment to standing up for yourself and others. Here are the steps you can take to confront and prevent workplace bullying:

- **GATHER YOUR EVIDENCE:** Document specific incidents with as much detail as possible, including the time, date, location, and—crucially—any other people who witnessed the incident.
- **CONFRONT THE INDIVIDUAL:** If you feel safe and comfortable doing so, approach the person responsible for the bullying behavior and request to speak to them privately. Calmly and assertively express your concerns about their behavior and explain why it's not okay. There's a chance that the person may not be aware of the effect their behavior is having, so this is an important step before escalating it further.
- **SEEK SUPPORT:** If the person refuses to accept your concerns about their behavior or if you don't feel comfortable speaking to them yourself, reach out to your mentor, boss, HR professionals, or workplace counselors. Remember, your workplace has a duty of care to you, and there are policies and employment laws in place to protect you.
- **STOP BULLYING IN ITS TRACKS:** Make sure that your actions, words, and behavior are contributing to an environment where bullying isn't allowed to fester in the first place. Make it clear that you have zero tolerance for bullying behavior and be a vocal advocate for respect, inclusivity, and accountability.

Making sure your voice is heard

In the competitive, bustling, fast-paced world of work, it can often feel like the only way to get ahead is to be the loudest voice in the room. This can be particularly challenging for those of us who are more introverted and struggle to speak up and assert ourselves—especially when we're just starting out in the professional world. While introversion is a valuable trait, it can sometimes hold us back when it comes to sharing our opinions and ideas, but with a bit of practice and these helpful tips, you can build the confidence to make sure your voice is heard.

THE WALLFLOWER'S GUIDE TO THE WORKPLACE

* EMBRACE IT: Introversion is not a flaw or a limitation, it's actually an invaluable aspect of your personality. Embrace your introverted nature and acknowledge the unique strengths it brings— such as deep thinking, creativity, and empathy—so you can leverage these powers to thrive in the workplace.

* PREPARE AND PLAN: Before participating in a meeting, presentation, or social event, take time to prepare and organize your thoughts. Anticipate the topics that will be discussed and consider your contributions in advance. Jot down key elements or ideas you want to express and practice articulating them aloud or in writing to build your confidence.

* FIND YOUR VOICE: In group settings, it can often be challenging to find opportunities to speak up and share your ideas. Start by actively listening to others and identifying moments where you can contribute relevantly to the conversation. When you have a point to make, speak calmly and assertively, focusing on the quality rather than the quantity of your contributions.

* NOURISH ONE-ON-ONE CONNECTIONS: Introverts often thrive in smaller groups where they can engage in deeper, more meaningful conversations. Take advantage of opportunities to connect with colleagues on a one-on-one basis, whether through coffee breaks, working lunches, or informal chats. Strengthening these personal connections can help build your confidence to express yourself in larger settings.

* RESPECT YOUR BOUNDARIES: Understand your comfort levels and set boundaries to preserve your energy and well-being. It's okay to decline invitations to social events or networking activities if they feel overwhelming or draining. Give yourself time to recharge your social battery so you can bring your best self to the next workplace setting.

Most of us aren't 100% extroverted or introverted, so we all have a bit of introversion in us.

Why it's totally okay to not know what you want

If you answered all the questions on page 32 with, "Umm . . . I don't know," then don't stress, this advice is for you. If you have no idea which path you want to take or feel overwhelmed by the pressure to have it all figured out, just know that you're not alone, this is totally normal and—plot twist—it might actually be a good thing.

> According to recent surveys, we're pretty comfortable with job hopping until we find what we want. 75 percent of Gen Z workers have reported changing jobs due to dissatisfaction, compared to 59 percent of millennials and 57 percent of Gen Xers. Good for us.

THE BENEFITS OF FIGURING IT OUT

- YOU GET TO TRY DIFFERENT THINGS: Dipping your toes in lots of different industries and roles will not only help you figure out what you want to do but will also greatly expand your skill set, build your confidence, and make you a well-rounded, unique, and interesting candidate when you eventually find a job you really want to apply for.

- YOU LEARN FROM YOUR MISTAKES: Finding your dream job is often a process of trial and error, and each experience—especially the unsuccessful ones—offers valuable lessons and insights that can guide your future decisions (knowing what you don't want is just as valuable as knowing what you do want!).

- YOU MEET LOTS OF DIFFERENT TYPES OF PEOPLE: Whether it's through trying several different jobs, volunteering, or traveling, you'll meet lots more people on the road less traveled than if you stick to one narrow path. And who knows, each new person you meet could inspire you to explore something you'd never thought of before or become a useful networking contact when you do figure it out.

- YOU LEARN VALUABLE SOFT SKILLS: As well as all the practical skills you'll pick up as you move about trying out different industries and roles, you'll also rack up a hefty number of impressive soft skills that you can only get from good old-fashioned life experience. Taking your time to sample everything life has to offer will make you more resilient, open-minded, adaptable, empathetic, confident, *and* more curious than most, and this can go a long way to helping you stand out from the crowd when you do eventually go for that dream job.

"I don't need to have it all figured out to move forward."

Employment versus self-employment

Whatever career you choose, as you embark on your journey you may find yourself weighing the pros and cons of different employment options. Whether you're comforted by the stability of traditional salaried employment or lured by the freedom of working for yourself, each path offers unique advantages and challenges. Let's dive into the pros and cons of both options so you can make an informed decision.

THE PROS AND CONS OF SALARIED EMPLOYMENT

PROS	CONS
JOB SECURITY: Salaried employment often provides a sense of stability and security, with a consistent paycheck and benefits package.	**LIMITED FLEXIBILITY:** You may have less flexibility in your work hours and schedule, with set expectations for office attendance and availability.
BENEFITS AND SUPPORT: Many employers offer comprehensive benefits packages, including health insurance, retirement plans, paid time off, and professional development opportunities.	**LESS AUTONOMY:** Salaried positions often come with a hierarchy of authority, requiring you to follow established protocols and seek approval for major decisions.
STRUCTURE AND STABILITY: Salaried positions typically come with a structured work schedule, defined roles and responsibilities, and opportunities for advancement within the organization.	**POTENTIAL FOR BURNOUT:** The demands of salaried positions, such as long hours and high expectations, can lead to burnout and work-related stress if you're not careful.

THE PROS AND CONS OF SELF-EMPLOYMENT

PROS	CONS
FLEXIBILITY: Working for yourself offers unparalleled flexibility in setting your own schedule, choosing your clients or customers, and determining your workload.	**LACK OF BENEFITS:** Unlike salaried positions, self-employed individuals are responsible for their own benefits, such as health insurance, retirement savings, and time off.
AUTONOMY: As a self-employed individual, you have full control over your business decisions, creative direction, and strategic planning.	**RESPONSIBILITY AND RISK:** Running a business comes with significant responsibility and risk, including managing your finances, securing clients or customers, and navigating legal and regulatory requirements.
UNLIMITED EARNING POTENTIAL: Self-employment allows you to directly benefit from your hard work and entrepreneurial efforts, with the possibility for unlimited earning potential.	**FINANCIAL INSECURITY:** Self-employment may come with financial instability, especially in the early stages of building your business or during economic downturns. Just as there's no upper limit to what you can earn, there's also no guarantee you'll earn anything at all.

Side hustles

Whether you just want to earn some extra cash or test the waters to see if you can turn your passion project into a full-time employment, it's never been easier to launch a profitable side hustle. Ready to dive headfirst into building your side hustle empire? Here's everything you need to know . . .

WHY YOU'LL LOVE A SIDE HUSTLE

1. **EXTRA CASH (OBVIOUSLY):** Need a little boost to your bank account? Your side hustle could become a little money-making machine to help you reach your savings goals faster than you can say "cha-ching!"

2. **FLEXIBILITY:** Unlike your regular nine-to-five gig, side hustles are usually pretty flexible, which means you can squeeze them in around your job, study, and social life.

3. **BOOST YOUR SKILLS:** Side hustles are a great way to learn new skills, beef up your résumé, and impress future employers with your entrepreneurial expertise.

HOW TO PICK YOUR HUSTLE BY YOUR PERSONALITY TYPE

- **ANIMAL LOVER:** If you can't get enough of our furry friends, why not start a dog-walking or pet-sitting business? Spending time with adorable animals and getting paid for it? It's a win-win!

- **TECH WHIZ:** If you're the go-to person for fixing tech problems or setting up gadgets for your friends and family, why not cast the net a little wider and offer your tech support services to the local community?

- **CRAFTY CREATIVE:** Got a knack for making cool stuff? Open an online shop selling your handmade crafts, artwork, or custom creations. You could even have a stand at your local market to show off your wares in person!

- **SOCIAL MEDIA SAVVY:** If you were born to rule the socials, why not offer social media management services to small businesses or influencers looking to up their online game?

- **FITNESS FANATIC:** Love breaking a sweat? Become a fitness instructor, personal trainer, or online coach to help others crush their fitness goals while you work on your own gains (and get paid for it!).

- **WORDSMITH:** If you're always discovering spelling mistakes in menus, uncovering errors in emails, or cringing at misplaced commas, you might just make a fabulous freelance proofreader.

- **TIP-TOP TEACHER:** Perhaps you had a favorite subject at school that you never got to utilize when adulthood arrived. You could find an opportunity to not only indulge your interests, but impart them onto someone else by tutoring, either online or in person.

However, don't let your side hustle take over your life! Set boundaries, schedule downtime, and remember to give yourself regular breaks to maintain your work/life balance.

Taking a career break

Even if you're relatively new to the workforce, it's never too early to start thinking about taking a break – especially if you've gone straight from full-time student into full-time work. A sabbatical allows you to do just that. It's essentially hitting pause on your regular work grind and taking an extended break to recharge, explore, and do all the things you've been daydreaming about during your daily commute. Read on to find out why a sabbatical might just be the ultimate power move for both your mental health and your career game.

FIRST OFF, WHAT'S A SABBATICAL?

A sabbatical is like a mini-retirement (minus the pullovers and bingo nights). It's a planned break from your usual job responsibilities that can last anywhere from a few weeks to a whole year, and they can be paid or unpaid. Think of it as your chance to hit the reset button on life and focus on personal growth, travel, passion projects, or just chilling out without the pressure of work.

HOW A SABBATICAL CAN BOOST YOUR MENTAL HEALTH

- REFRESH, RECHARGE, REJUVENATE: Picture this: no emails, no deadlines, no office drama. Sounds dreamy, right? A sabbatical gives you the time and space to decompress, destress, and reconnect with what truly brings you joy.

- MINDFUL ME-TIME: Use your sabbatical to pin down those self-care habits you've been putting off. Whether it's getting into meditation, going on solo adventures, or starting your fitness journey, do whatever brings you joy and nourishes your soul.

- GET YOUR CREATIVE JUICES FLOWING: Stepping away from your routine can spark inspiration like nobody's business. Use your sabbatical to finally write that book, pick up a paintbrush, or delve into any of the other creative pursuits you've been eager to try out.

HOW TO SELL THE IDEA OF A SABBATICAL TO YOUR EMPLOYER

- HAPPY, HEALTHY EMPLOYEES: Here's a secret: happy, well-rested employees are more productive, engaged, and loyal—pass it on! By offering sabbatical opportunities, employers can boost morale, reduce burnout, and create a workplace culture that values work-life balance.

- IT'S ALL ABOUT RETENTION: If an employer wants to keep their star players (like you) around for the long haul, offering sabbaticals is a surefire way to retain top talent and build an army of loyal, committed team players who aren't desperate to jump ship.

- FRESH PERSPECTIVES: Ever come back from vacation full of brilliant ideas? Imagine that, but magnified by a million. Sabbaticals give employees the chance to gain fresh perspectives, develop new skills, and bring innovative ideas back to the table, which gives the company a unique edge and benefits everyone in the long run.

Thinking of a career change?

Embarking on a career change can be both exhilarating and daunting. Whether you're feeling stuck in your current job, seeking new challenges, or finally pursuing your passion, switching careers requires careful consideration, patience, and understanding.

WHAT TO CONSIDER BEFORE A CAREER CHANGE

You might enjoy this . . .	But there's also this . . .
PERSONAL GROWTH AND FULFILLMENT: A career change that more closely aligns your work with your values, interests, and passions can greatly improve your well-being and sense of purpose.	**A TEST OF STRENGTH:** A career change may involve setbacks, rejections, or failures along the way, putting your resilience, perseverance, and determination to the test.
INCREASED JOB SATISFACTION: Moving to a new career path that resonates with you can lead to you feeling more satisfied, motivated, and enthusiastic about your work.	**AN AWKWARD TRANSITION PERIOD:** Transitioning to a new career path can be challenging and may require a period of adjustment, retraining, and networking before achieving stability and success.
PROFESSIONAL DEVELOPMENT: Switching careers can open doors to acquiring new skills, knowledge, and experiences, which will enhance your professional development and marketability.	**ONE STEP FORWARD, TWO STEPS BACK:** Switching careers may mean starting from the bottom or stepping back in terms of seniority, status, or recognition within your new field.
IMPROVED WORK-LIFE BALANCE: A carefully planned career change might lead to flexible hours, remote work options, or reduced stress levels.	**PERSONAL STRESS:** A career change can have ripple effects on your personal life, relationships, and lifestyle as you navigate the new chapter in your career.
HIGHER EARNING POTENTIAL: In some cases, a career change can lead to higher earning potential, especially if you're transitioning to a field with greater demand or higher salaries.	**FINANCIAL FLUCTUATIONS:** Changing careers can have a domino effect on your finances, especially if you have to take a pay cut or invest in retraining or additional qualifications.

Whatever your reason for a career change, the more you prepare, the more likely you'll be to enjoy a smooth transition. Start saving up in case you need to take a pay cut, spruce up your résumé and LinkedIn profile, and finally: research, research, research!

"The only way to do great work is to love what you do. If you haven't found it yet, keep looking. Don't settle."

STEVE JOBS

Asking for a pay raise or promotion

If you've been hitting all the right notes lately by smashing your targets, getting great feedback, and making moves to progress in your role, you might have your eye on a pay raise or promotion. But if the idea of sitting down in front of your boss and asking for more money or a better title makes you break out in hives, don't worry, we're going to walk you through the process with only minimal uncomfortable itching.

HOW TO NAVIGATE A PAY RAISE OR PROMOTION

- DO YOUR RESEARCH: Yessss, we know. We say this every time. But if you fail to prepare, you prepare to fail. Before having a conversation with your boss, arm yourself with as much information about industry standards and the value of your role as you can. Research comparable positions and salary ranges to support your request.

- HIGHLIGHT YOUR ACHIEVEMENTS: Prepare documentation of your accomplishments, outlining tangible results and contributions you've made to the company. Quantify your successes wherever possible to demonstrate the impact of your efforts.

- PRACTICE YOUR PITCH: Rehearse your talking points and anticipate potential objections or questions from your manager. Present your case confidently, emphasizing how a pay raise or promotion aligns with your skills, experience, and commitment to the organization.

- FOCUS ON VALUE: Frame your request in terms of the value you bring to the company rather than solely focusing on your personal needs or desires. Highlight how investing in your growth and development will benefit the organization in the long run.

- BE FLEXIBLE: Keep an open mind during negotiations and be willing to compromise if necessary. Explore alternative forms of compensation or opportunities for advancement if an immediate salary increase or promotion isn't feasible.

- FOLLOW UP: After the initial discussion, follow up with your manager to express gratitude for their time and reaffirm your commitment to your professional development. Continue to demonstrate your value through ongoing performance and contributions.

What do you do if they say no? If there's a reason why your request can't be considered right now, ask if you can circle back to it in 3, 6 or 12 months, or whenever the situation has changed. If it's a flat not-now-not-ever, at least you know where you stand and you can start looking for better opportunities elsewhere.

Navigating workplace politics

Oh, workplace politics. This might be one of the few realities of adult life that school actually prepared us for by laying the groundwork. It's a small leap from, "Ali copied my answers in the geography quiz," and "It's not fair, I always get picked last for sports," to "Mark claimed credit for my ideas in that presentation," and "It's not fair, I always get overlooked for promotions." Just like in the classroom, navigating these dynamics in the workplace can be a tricky business, but with some well-coordinated steps, you can learn how to dance around office politics like a pro.

THE WORKPLACE POLITICS DANCE

- STAY NEUTRAL: Avoid getting caught up in workplace gossip or problematic conversations that could compromise your reputation. Keep your interactions positive and steer clear of taking sides in workplace conflicts.

- READ THE ROOM: Take note of the power dynamics and relationships within your organization. Be mindful of influential players and alliances that may impact decision-making processes.

As well as the official organizational hierarchy, in most workplaces, if you look closely, you'll also notice an unofficial hierarchy. This is likely based on personal friendships, histories, and connections—recognizing this can be useful for knowing where the power really lies in the organization.

- KEEP IT PROFESSIONAL: Treat everyone with respect and professionalism. Avoid engaging in behaviors or conversations that could be considered unprofessional or inappropriate.

- FOCUS ON YOUR GOALS: Stay focused on your professional objectives and avoid getting distracted by office politics. Keep your eye on the prize and work toward achieving your goals, regardless of any workplace dynamics.

- BUILD RELATIONSHIPS: Cultivate positive relationships by getting to know the key stakeholders and decision-makers within your organization. Offer your assistance and expertise when appropriate and seek out trusted mentors who can provide guidance and support.

- KNOW WHEN TO STEP BACK: If you find yourself embroiled in office drama or conflict, know when to step back and focus on your own work. Avoid getting drawn into unnecessary conflicts or power struggles that could derail your career progress.

How to network like a pro

You've probably heard it before (in fact, you've definitely already read it in this book), but networking is essential if you want to kickstart your career progression, boost your development opportunities, and generally expand your contact list of awesome people you can call on both inside and outside your industry. Here's how to build your own social network from scratch (move over Zuckerberg, there's a new kid in town).

BUILD YOUR OWN SOCIAL NETWORK

1. **EXPAND YOUR HORIZONS:** Don't limit yourself to networking within your immediate circle. Explore different avenues such as industry events, online forums, and professional associations to connect with a diverse range of individuals.

2. **FOCUS ON AUTHENTIC CONNECTIONS:** Approach networking with sincerity and authenticity. Instead of focusing solely on what others can do for you, strive to build genuine relationships based on mutual interests and shared values.

3. **LEAVE A LASTING IMPRESSION:** Be polite, purposeful, and—more importantly—interested. Ask lots of questions and engage with genuine curiosity. Jump ahead to page 157 to pick up some tips for how to make small talk that will ensure you never have an awkward encounter again.

4. **FOLLOW UP WITH PURPOSE:** After making a connection, don't let it fade into the background. Follow up promptly with a personalized message to express your gratitude and interest in maintaining the connection. Be proactive in nurturing your new connection to enjoy a more fruitful relationship.

5. **GIVE AS YOU RECEIVE:** Networking is a two-way street. Be generous with your time, knowledge, and resources, and offer support to others whenever possible. Building a reputation as a helpful and reliable professional will enhance your networking efforts in the long run.

Actively chase networking opportunities on a regular basis—such as aiming to reach out to one new contact a week on LinkedIn, attending one online event each month, or simply making an effort to mingle more widely at after-work drinks.

Email etiquette

Love it or hate it, emailing is still one of the most common forms of communication in the workplace, and now that many more of us are working remotely, it's more important than ever to acquire the art of tactful written communication. We ran some common phrases through the Email Etiquette Translation Machine so you can show that you're just as professional, assertive, and impressive in writing as you are in person.

THE EMAIL ETIQUETTE TRANSLATION MACHINE

WHAT YOU WANT TO SAY . . .	WHAT YOU SAY INSTEAD . . .
"Sorry for the delayed reply."	"Thank you for your patience."
"I hope that makes sense!"	"Please let me know if you have any questions."
"I'll get back to you ASAP!"	"I'll aim to respond to you by [specific time/date]."
"There's no way I can do this."	"Let me explore alternative options."
"I'm too busy right now."	"I'm currently managing multiple tasks, but I'll prioritize your request and provide an update by [insert time/date]."
"I have no idea what you're talking about."	"Thank you for your email. Could you please provide more details?"
"Yeah . . . that's not my problem."	"I'm happy to help you resolve this issue. Let me know how I can assist."
"I NEED THIS ASAP!"	"Could you please prioritize this request?"
"Yes, I got your email, please stop chasing me."	"Thank you for your email. I'll be in touch as soon as I have an update."
"I'm really not comfortable with this."	"I have some concerns about this approach. Can we discuss this further?"

The art of delegating

One common workplace hurdle is the desire to try and do everything yourself, especially when you're young and hungry to prove yourself in a new role or organization. But sharing the load and grasping the art of delegating is essential if you want to truly boost your productivity, build collaboration skills, and gain peace of mind.

WHAT IS DELEGATION?

Delegation is similar to assembling a crew for a ship. It's all about entrusting certain tasks to others and allowing them to handle certain responsibilities so you can focus on steering the ship toward success. Knowing how and when to delegate is crucial in the workplace—it's the difference between smooth sailing and a shipwreck.

WHY SHOULD YOU DELEGATE?

1. **BOOST PRODUCTIVITY:** Delegating frees up your time to focus on the tasks that require your specific expertise, speeding up overall progress and letting you use your time and energy more effectively (which leads to greater job satisfaction—it really is a win-win!).

2. **FOSTER COLLABORATION:** By involving others in tasks, you build a greater sense of teamwork and collaboration, which can sometimes inspire innovative solutions you wouldn't otherwise have uncovered and stronger relationships all round.

3. **PREVENT BURNOUT:** Distributing tasks evenly prevents you from feeling overwhelmed, reduces stress, and promotes a healthier work-life balance. Plus, if you need to take time off from work, you can rest easy knowing other people can pick up the slack while you're away.

TIPS FOR EFFECTIVE DELEGATION

- **IDENTIFY TASKS:** Determine which tasks can be delegated without compromising quality or deadlines.

- **CHOOSE THE RIGHT PERSON:** Assign tasks to individuals with the necessary skills and knowledge to complete them successfully.

- **COMMUNICATE CLEARLY:** Provide clear instructions, expectations, and deadlines to avoid misunderstandings.

- **OFFER SUPPORT:** Be available to answer questions, provide guidance, and offer assistance as needed.

- **TRUST AND EMPOWER:** Trust your team members to complete the tasks effectively and empower them to make decisions within their scope of responsibility.

- **PROVIDE FEEDBACK:** Offer constructive feedback on completed tasks to encourage growth and improvement.

Making the most of your commute

If you're traveling into work every day, your commute doesn't have to be a mindless, scrolling snooze-fest. Manage this time and turn it into an opportunity to learn, grow, and generally make the most of your downtime. Who knows? Your next big idea or breakthrough moment might just happen during your daily commute . . .

WAYS TO SPEND YOUR COMMUTE THAT AREN'T PHONE SCROLLING

- **DIVE INTO A PODCAST:** Whether you're into true crime mysteries, mind-blowing science, or a good giggle, there's a podcast out there with your name on it.
- **COMMUTE TO THE BEAT:** If you like listening to music during your commutes, why not switch up your playlist and explore new music genres? Now's your chance to broaden your musical horizons and become the ultimate music connoisseur.
- **GET LOST IN A GOOD BOOK:** If you're lucky enough to snag a seat on public transport, why not crack open a book and let your imagination soar? Whether it's a classic novel, a self-help gem, or a thrilling mystery, there's nothing like a good read to make your commute fly by. (Hint: if you don't want to lug a heavy book around all day, why not get yourself an e-reader? It's like carrying a featherlight library with you everywhere you go!)
- **GET LINGUISTIC WITH IT:** ¡Hola! Bonjour! Nǐ hǎo! Turn your commute into a a private communication class with a language-learning app and impress your friends (and the person peering over your shoulder on the train) with your newfound linguistic prowess.
- **A COURSE, OF COURSE!:** Transform your commute into a mini classroom by listening to an audio course or lecture. From history and psychology to business and technology, there's an audio course out there for every interest and passion.
- **HAVE A MINDFUL MOMENT:** Use your commute as an opportunity to unwind, meditate, or practice deep breathing exercises. It's the perfect way to get into the right headspace to start the day or decompress on the way home so you can enjoy your evening and leave your rage on the road.
- **CREATIVE CORNER:** Get your creative juices flowing by brainstorming ideas or jotting down your thoughts in a journal. Whether you're plotting your next novel, doodling in a sketchbook, or writing song lyrics, let your creativity run wild during your commute.
- **AUDIOBOOK ADVENTURE:** Do you love to read but don't have your hands free while you're commuting? Enter, audiobooks. All the joy of a good story without having to lift a finger (or turn a page).

Finding balance in a workaholic world

In our fast-paced, always-plugged-in society, there's often an unspoken expectation that we'll be available to answer work emails or calls at any time of the day, or work late into the night and sacrifice our weekends in the name of being a "team player." But here's the truth: burnout is real, and constantly pushing yourself to the limit is neither sustainable nor healthy. Let's find out why it's so important to physically and mentally switch off from work.

> Contrary to popular belief, working around the clock doesn't make you a better employee—it just makes you exhausted. It's essential to recognize that downtime is not a luxury, but a necessity for maintaining your physical health and mental well-being.

THE ART OF SWITCHING OFF
Here are some simple tips to help you disconnect from work and recharge your batteries:

- **SET BOUNDARIES:** Establish clear boundaries between your work and personal time. Make it clear that you don't check emails or take work calls outside of your designated hours and stand your ground—if you answer the odd email or call after hours here and there, before you know it, you'll be expected to do it all the time . . .
- **UNPLUG TECHNOLOGY:** Power down your devices and step away from screens during your downtime. Engage in activities that don't involve technology, such as reading, cooking, or spending time outdoors.
- **PRACTICE MINDFULNESS:** Incorporate mindfulness techniques into your daily routine, such as meditation or deep breathing exercises. These practices can help reduce stress and promote relaxation.
- **PRIORITIZE SELF-CARE:** Make self-care a priority by scheduling regular exercise, adequate sleep, and activities that bring you joy. Remember, self-care is not selfish—it's essential for your overall well-being.
- **PLAN LEISURE ACTIVITIES:** Fill your weekends and evenings with activities that rejuvenate you (and, crucially, take your mind off work), whether it's spending time with loved ones, pursuing hobbies, or exploring new interests.

EMBRACE THE POWER OF REST
In a culture that glorifies busyness, don't ignore the importance of rest and relaxation. By prioritizing self-care and setting boundaries around work, you can achieve a healthier balance and thrive both personally and professionally. So go ahead, give yourself permission to switch off, recharge, and enjoy the precious moments of life outside of work. Your well-rested self will thank you for it!

Knowing when it's time to walk away

In the journey of life, we often find ourselves at a crossroads, faced with the daunting decision of whether to continue down our current path or veer off in a new direction. Adulthood is full of these moments, but when it comes to our careers, knowing when it's time to quit can be a particularly challenging and often emotional process. But here's the truth: it's okay to walk away from a situation that no longer serves you, and recognizing the signs that it's time to move on is the first step toward finding greater fulfillment and happiness.

We spend approximately one-third of our lives at work, so it's essential that we spend that time doing enjoyable, meaningful work in a supportive environment.

THE WARNING SIGNS THAT IT'S TIME TO QUIT

- **YOU'VE LOST YOUR PASSION:** If you find yourself feeling apathetic or indifferent about your work, despite once feeling passionate about it, it may be a sign that what you're looking for from your job has changed.
- **YOU'RE ALWAYS STRESSED:** Chronic stress, anxiety, or feeling overwhelmed can take a significant toll on your mental and physical well-being. If your job consistently leaves you feeling drained or exhausted, it may be time to walk away.
- **YOU'RE NOT GOING ANYWHERE:** Feeling stagnant or stuck in your career growth can be frustrating and demoralizing. If your current job lacks opportunities for advancement or skill development, you may be better off seeking new challenges elsewhere.
- **YOU'RE IN A TOXIC WORK ENVIRONMENT:** A negative or toxic workplace culture can have a detrimental effect on your overall happiness and job satisfaction. If you find yourself surrounded by gossip, conflict, or hostility, move on.
- **YOU DON'T SHARE THE SAME VALUES:** If your values and beliefs clash with those of your employer or company culture, it can create a sense of disconnect and discomfort. Aligning yourself with an organization that shares your values might lead to a renewed sense of purpose.

HOW TO QUIT WITH GRACE

New message

To | manager@company.com

Subject | Resignation

"Dear [insert manager's name]

Please accept this as my formal resignation from [insert role] effective [x] weeks from this date. I would like to thank you for the opportunities you've provided me and for your support throughout my time in this role. I wish you and the company all the best for the future. Please let me know how I can contribute to a smooth transition period.

Best regards [name]"

Send

Finance

AKA THE FINANCE FERRIS WHEEL

As you make your way through Adult Land, you really can't miss the Finance Ferris Wheel looming large over the horizon, casting its imposing shadow over pretty much everything you do. Since you can't ignore it any longer, you may as well take a ride, but be warned—the highs are as exhilarating as the lows are devastating.

In this chapter, we'll ride the Finance Ferris Wheel to take a birds-eye view of all the essential money management tips, tricks, and terms you need to know in order to safeguard your current and future financial health and reach your savings goals—whatever they may be. Whether you want to understand the basics of budgeting, explore the different types of savings accounts, or learn the passive income hacks to make money in your sleep, this chapter is positively packed with handy advice, strategies, and step-by-step methods to help you become skilled at the art of money management.

As you take your turn on the Finance Ferris Wheel, please keep in mind that the information provided in this chapter is designed to offer general guidance on various financial topics. It's extremely important to note that the financial regulations, practices, and options available to you will vary depending on your location and personal circumstances, so make sure you do your research to tailor the tips and advice in this chapter to your situation.

The art of budgeting

Remember those carefree days when you'd splurge on the latest video game, new clothes, and trips to the movies without a second thought? Well, that was before your expensive one-way trip to Adult Land. Now, as the bills pile up and the reality of adult life sets in, that financial freedom is but a distant memory. These days, if you want to not only survive but thrive in the adult world, you really need to become an expert in budgeting—and *fast*.

WAIT, WHERE DID ALL MY MONEY GO?

If you only learn one lesson from your ride on the Finance Ferris Wheel, make sure it's the importance of budgeting. Budgeting isn't about depriving yourself of life's pleasures—it's about harnessing your spending power and directing it toward the things that truly matter. You'll learn all about budgeting in detail over the next couple of pages, but the basics are:

- Start by tracking your expenses and setting realistic goals for saving and spending.
- Create a budget that reflects your priorities, whether it's saving for a dream vacation or building an emergency fund.
- Don't forget to leave room for the occasional splurge (life is for living, after all).

"A budget is telling your money where to go instead of wondering where it went."—Dave Ramsey

THE 50/30/20 RULE

The 50/30/20 budgeting rule is a simple yet effective strategy for managing your finances. In essence, it suggests allocating 50 percent of your income to the essentials like housing, utilities, and groceries, 30 percent to all the fun stuff like dining out, entertainment, and shopping, and finally, 20 percent to sensible things like savings and debt repayment. This is a great rule to follow to help you achieve financial stability, security, and freedom over time.

How to save on a tight budget

When money's tight, this is when budgeting takes on a whole new level of importance. You'll need to make sure every penny counts (and is accounted for), so it's essential to get your budgeting down to a fine art. Let's look at the bare bones of what you should be saving when things are lean using the 50/30/20 model.

50 PERCENT NEEDS (ESSENTIALS)

- **HOUSING COSTS:** Make sure you have enough to cover your rent or mortgage payments each month.
- **BASIC LIVING EXPENSES:** What's left after your housing costs will go toward essentials like food, bills, transportation, and healthcare.
- **LOAN/DEBT REPAYMENTS:** Don't forget your minimum repayments for your student loan or any other loans or debt.

30 PERCENT WANTS (NICE-TO-HAVES)

- **STREAMING SUBSCRIPTIONS:** That's right, Netflix is not an essential!
- **ENTERTAINMENT:** Have a budget for things like theater trips, nights out, and dinners with your friends and stick to it each month.
- **PERSONAL CARE:** These are your haircuts, massages, gym memberships, and so on.
- **TRAVEL:** These are the trips outside your essential commutes, like mini getaways, weekend trips, and visits to see friends and family.

20 PERCENT SAVINGS (FOR A RAINY DAY)

- **EMERGENCY FUND:** For when it's really raining.
- **RETIREMENT SAVINGS:** Yep, you've got to start saving now.
- **BIG GOALS:** This could include buying a house, taking a trip, or saving up for a wedding.

TIPS FOR SAVING ON A TIGHT BUDGET

- **BE THRIFTY:** This one might seem obvious, but you could be overlooking some key areas where you can make unexpected savings. Jump ahead to page 155 to pick up some great tips on where you can shave pennies off your expenses by cutting out senseless spending.
- **HAVE AN EYE FOR A BARGAIN:** Look out for discounts, coupons, and special offers, and wait for key moments in the year (like Labor Day and Black Friday sales) to make big purchases. Research and download special apps and plugins which scour the web for hidden vouchers whenever you shop online.
- **DON'T SQUANDER WINDFALLS:** Tax refunds, work bonuses, birthday cash, or even little lottery wins might seem like perfect opportunities for frivolous purchases, but if you channel them into your savings account where they can grow and multiply, you'll be much better off in the long run.

How to save on a comfortable budget

Congratulations, you've hit a new milestone in your financial journey—the comfortable budget zone! Now that you're no longer pinching pennies, it's time to level up your budgeting game and explore some exciting new strategies for getting the most out of your hard-earned cash.

INTRODUCING "F*** OFF" FUNDS

Imagine having a financial safety net so comfy it's more like a cashmere weighted blanket. That's basically what a "f*** off" fund is! This fund is essentially a juicy little savings pot that gives you the peace of mind and financial freedom to say, "You know what, f*** off!" at any point in your life and walk away from a toxic situation without worrying about the financial implications. This could include turning your back on a housing situation that's become uncomfortable or saying *buh-bye* to a job that's destroying your soul. So, if you're making bank now, put some of it toward a "f*** off" fund and enjoy the warm, fuzzy feeling of financial freedom from sucky situations.

SAY HELLO TO SINKING FUNDS

Ever wished you could wave a magic wand and make those annual expenses disappear? Well, sinking funds are the next best thing! Sinking funds are a kind of savings account that lets you set aside money each month for predictable future expenses, like your annual ski trip, your pesky student loan, or your fur baby's vet bills.

RETHINK YOUR 50/30/20

Depending on your personal priorities and just how flush you are these days, what goes into each bucket of your 50/30/20 savings might shift a little. Here are some extra expenses you might want to make room for now that things are a little more comfortable.

- **DEBT REPAYMENT:** If you can afford it, consider knocking out any high-interest debt you're paying off. Always check your repayment plan to work out whether you're better off paying a lump sum or continuing to pay step-by-step.
- **INVESTMENTS:** Once you've covered the essentials, consider putting your money to work through investments like stocks, bonds, or real estate.
- **PASSION PROJECTS:** Whether it's getting into gaming, brewing your own beer, or trying your hand at hang-gliding, you can stretch your leisure a little further and indulge in some of those activities or hobbies you've always wanted to try.
- **A CAREER BREAK:** Back on page 41, you learned all about sabbaticals and career breaks. If you're lucky, your organization might offer a paid sabbatical scheme, but if not, putting aside enough money to tide you over if you want to take a break from work is definitely worth thinking about.
- **UPGRADES:** Whether you're thinking of renovating your bathroom, investing in an electric car, or just replacing your laptop with one that doesn't hum like a swarm of angry bees, why not use your extra cash to indulge in some upgrades?

Types of savings accounts

Bewildered by options when picking your savings account? It's understandable. There are lots of options out there, each with their own perks and potential for making your money work harder for you. Whether you're stockpiling cash for a rainy day, planning for your retirement, or saving up for specific goals, there's a savings account out there to suit your needs and help you reach your financial dreams!

SAVINGS ACCOUNT	HOW IT WORKS
Traditional/easy access savings	This is your basic savings account, offering a safe place to stash your cash with minimal risk. (This is probably the type of savings account you had as a kid.)
High-yield savings	This baby earns you higher interest rates than traditional savings, helping your money grow over time (*cha-ching*).
Money market	This combines the features of both checking and savings accounts, with potential for higher interest rates.
Certificate of deposit (CD)	This one locks in your money for a set period, typically offering higher interest rates in return.
Individual retirement account (IRA) or personal savings account (PSA)	These are tax-advantaged accounts designed for retirement savings, with various investment options. (Tax-advantaged just means you get some tax benefits.)
Health savings account (HSA)	This account is specifically to help you save for medical expenses, with tax benefits and the option to invest for growth.
Education savings account (ESA)	This one is designed to help you save for education expenses, offering tax advantages for qualified withdrawals.

Remember, depending on your location and personal circumstances, not every type of savings account will be applicable or available to you.

All about investing

Think investing is just for Wall Street tycoons in fancy suits? Think again! Anyone can get into investing, all it takes is a little research, some basic knowledge, and a willingness to learn. So, if you've ever dreamed of dabbling in the world of investing but have absolutely no idea where to start, this is the page for you. Buckle up, moneybags, because we're about to show you how investing can make your money work for you!

DISCLAIMER: BEFORE WE DIVE INTO THE FUN STUFF, A QUICK WORD OF CAUTION: Investing comes with risks, and there are absolutely no guarantees of returns. Always do your own thorough research and consult with a financial advisor before making any investment decisions.

WHAT ACTUALLY IS INVESTING?
Investing is like planting seeds in a garden, but instead of flowers, you're growing your money! It's all about putting your hard-earned cash into assets like stocks, bonds, or real estate with the hope of earning a return on your investment over time.

TIPS FOR BEGINNER INVESTORS
- EDUCATE YOURSELF: Read books, listen to podcasts, and devour online resources to learn the ins and outs of investing.

- START SMALL: This is not a go-big-or-go-home kind of endeavor. Experiment with low-cost options like index funds or exchange-traded funds (ETFs) before making any big moves.

- SET GOALS: Figure out what you're investing for—whether it's retirement, a dream vacation, or just to get into a more comfortable financial situation—and tailor your investment strategy accordingly.

- DIVERSIFY: Don't put all your eggs in one basket! Diversify your investments across different asset classes to minimize risk.

- STAY CALM: Investing can be a rollercoaster ride, with plenty of ups and downs along the way. Keep a cool head and resist the urge to panic-sell when the market takes a dip.

Over the long-term, stocks have historically provided higher returns compared to other investment options like bonds or savings accounts. According to data from the S&P 500 Index, stocks have returned an average of around 7-10 percent annually over the past century.

Stocks and shares

If you find yourself nodding along vacantly when people talk about stocks and shares, don't worry, you're definitely not the only one. The terms "stocks" and "shares" are often used interchangeably, but they refer to slightly different concepts in the context of investing, so let's break them both down and see how you can dip your toes into stocks and shares without too many shocks and scares.

WHAT ARE STOCKS AND SHARES?

Think of stocks and shares as tiny slices of ownership in a company's pie. When you buy stocks or shares, you're essentially buying a piece of the company's profits (and losses). "Stocks" typically refer to ownership in a company, while "shares" can also refer to ownership in other assets, like mutual funds or ETFs. Stocks are traded on stock exchanges, and shares can be held by investors as part of their investment portfolio.

ALL ABOUT STOCKS

Stocks are typically traded on stock exchanges, such as the New York Stock Exchange (NYSE), the Nasdaq Stock Market, and the London Stock Exchange (LSE), where investors buy and sell shares of publicly traded companies.

Examples of stocks include:

- Apple Inc. (AAPL)
- Amazon.com Inc. (AMZN)
- Alphabet Inc. (GOOGL)
- Microsoft Corporation (MSFT)
- Tesla, Inc. (TSLA).

ALL ABOUT SHARES

- Shares refer to units of ownership in a specific company. Each share represents a portion of ownership in the company's assets and earnings.
- When a company issues shares, it divides its ownership into equal portions and sells them to investors (like you) in exchange for capital (your money). For example, if you own 100 shares of Apple Inc., you own 100 units of ownership in Apple.

HOW TO GET STARTED

Follow the tips for beginner investors from the previous page and remember to start small and stick to well-established, large-scale companies with a proven track record (think household names like Apple, Amazon, or Coca-Cola). Purchase a small amount of stock and monitor its performance over time. This will give you a feel for how the market works without risking too much of your hard-earned cash.

Insurance

Back on page 16, you learned about the ins and outs of home insurance, but there are a few other types of insurance you need to know about in your new adult life. Depending on your lifestyle, some of these may not be relevant to you right now, but it's worth taking a few minutes to understand your options when it comes to protecting yourself and your valuables against life's unexpected curveballs.

THE DIFFERENT TYPES OF INSURANCE

- **CAR INSURANCE:** Whether you're sputtering around town in a junker on wheels or cruising in a sleek dream machine, car insurance is a must-have to protect yourself and others on the road. Make sure you have adequate coverage for your vehicle's value and your driving habits.

- **LIFE INSURANCE:** Life insurance provides financial security for your loved ones in the event that anything should happen to you.

- **TRAVEL INSURANCE:** Planning a dream vacay? Don't forget to pack your travel insurance! It can cover unexpected mishaps like trip cancellations, lost luggage, or medical emergencies abroad, giving you peace of mind wherever you wander.

- **PET INSURANCE:** Your fur babies need protection too! Pet insurance helps cover veterinary bills and medical expenses for your beloved furry, feathered, or scaly companions. From routine check-ups to unexpected surgeries, pet insurance ensures your pets get the care they need without breaking the bank.

HOW TO MAKE SURE YOU STAY INSURED

- **SET REMINDERS:** Life gets busy, but don't let insurance slip through the cracks! Set calendar reminders or alerts on your phone to notify you when your premiums are due or policies need renewal.

- **AUTOMATE PAYMENTS:** You've got enough to think about, so take remembering to pay for insurance off your plate by setting up automatic withdrawals from your bank account.

- **REVIEW REGULARLY:** As your life changes, so will your insurance needs. Periodically review your policies to ensure they still align with your current circumstances and make adjustments as necessary (perhaps make it part of your yearly life review).

- **BUNDLE UP:** Consider bundling multiple insurance policies with the same provider to take advantage of discounts and streamline your coverage. It's a win-win for your wallet and your peace of mind!

A tax crash course

Ah, taxes—the inevitable rite of passage into adulthood. While they may not be the most thrilling topic, you really can't (and definitely shouldn't) avoid them. So, make an extra-large coffee and grab your calculators as we get to grips with the facts about tax.

THE FACTS ABOUT TAX

- **THEY FUND PUBLIC SERVICES:** Taxes play a vital role in funding essential public services that we all use, like education, healthcare, infrastructure, and public safety. They ensure that everyone has access to vital resources and services that contribute to a functioning society.

- **THEY CONTRIBUTE TO THE REDISTRIBUTION OF WEATH:** Taxes help redistribute wealth by imposing higher taxes on those with higher incomes and providing support to those in need through social welfare programs. This helps promote economic equality and social cohesion within our communities.

- **THEY PROVIDE ECONOMIC STABILITY:** Taxation is also used as a tool for economic stability, with governments adjusting tax rates to manage inflation, stimulate economic growth, and regulate consumer behavior.

DIFFERENT TYPES OF TAXES

(note: not all of these may apply to you or your country)

1. **INCOME TAX:** This is typically calculated as a percentage of your total income.

2. **SALES TAX:** This is imposed on the sale of goods and services and is typically added at the point of purchase.

3. **PROPERTY TAX:** This is levied on the value of real estate properties owned by individuals or businesses.

4. **VALUE-ADDED TAX (VAT) OR GOODS AND SERVICES TAX (GST):** VAT/GST is a consumption tax applied to the value added at each stage of production or distribution of goods and services.

5. **CORPORATE TAX:** Corporations are subject to corporate tax on their profits.

HOW TO MANAGE YOUR TAX

- **KNOW YOUR OBLIGATIONS:** You're responsible for understanding your tax obligations based on your income, employment status, and location. Stay informed about tax deadlines and requirements to avoid penalties or fines.

- **SEEK PROFESSIONAL ADVICE:** Tax laws and regulations can be super complex and ever-changing, so don't hesitate to seek guidance from tax professionals or financial advisors.

- **KEEP RECORDS:** Get into the habit of keeping organized records of your income, expenses, and deductions throughout the year to streamline the tax filing process (if this applies to you personally) and ensure accuracy.

The best bank account for you

If you've had the same bank account since you were 11, it might be time to start thinking about other bank account options to suit your changing financial needs as you move into adulthood. Whether you're looking for convenience, high-interest earnings, or rewards perks, let's explore your banking options to find the best fit for you.

CHECKING ACCOUNTS ARE GREAT FOR . . .

- EVERYDAY SPENDING: A checking account is your go-to for daily transactions like groceries, bills, and dining out. With features like debit cards, online banking, and mobile apps, checking accounts offer convenience and accessibility.

- NO-FEE OPTIONS: Many banks offer fee-free checking accounts with no minimum balance requirements, making them ideal for young adults or those just starting their financial journey (hence why you probably had this type of account as a kid).

- DIRECT DEPOSITS: You can set up direct deposits for your regular incoming (i.e., your paycheck) and outgoing (i.e., your bills and subscriptions) expenses.

REWARDS CHECKING ACCOUNTS ARE GREAT FOR . . .

- GETTING CASHBACK: Rewards checking accounts offer perks like cashback on debit card purchases, making them a lucrative option for everyday spending.

- EARNING POINTS OR MILES: Some banks partner with airlines or retailers to offer rewards points or miles for qualifying purchases, allowing you to earn discounts or freebies on future purchases.

SAVINGS ACCOUNTS ARE GREAT FOR . . .

- EMERGENCY FUNDS: A savings account is your safety net for unexpected expenses or emergencies. Aim to set aside three to six months' worth of living expenses to weather any financial storms.

- INTEREST EARNINGS: Unlike checking accounts, savings accounts typically earn interest on your deposits, helping your money grow over time. Look for accounts with competitive interest rates to maximize your earnings (free money, yay!).

- AUTOMATED SAVINGS: You can set up automatic transfers from your checking account to your savings account to build your nest egg over time without even thinking about it.

HIGH-YIELD SAVINGS ACCOUNTS ARE GREAT FOR . . .

- HIGHER INTEREST RATES: High-yield savings accounts offer significantly higher interest rates than traditional savings accounts, allowing your money to work harder for you (even *more* free money, yay!).

- SMARTER BANKING: Many online banks offer high-yield savings accounts with no monthly fees and competitive interest rates. Explore online banking options to find the best rates and terms for your savings goals.

The ins and outs of borrowing

Buying something on credit/layaway or taking out a loan is basically the next-level adult-y version of borrowing a bit of cash from your family to help out when money is tight. From making everyday purchases to financing big-ticket items, let's look at the ins and outs of borrowing responsibly.

ALL ABOUT CREDIT

- BORROWING POWER: Credit allows you to borrow money with the promise that you'll pay it back later. It's like getting an advance on your paycheck (except from a financial institution instead of your boss).

- WATCH OUT FOR YOUR CREDIT SCORE: Your credit score is like your financial report card— it reflects your borrowing history and lets lenders assess your creditworthiness. Maintain a good credit score by keeping up to date with your repayments and keeping debt low.

BUYING ON LAYAWAY

- FLEXIBLE PAYMENTS: Buying something on layaway allows you to spread out the cost of a big-ticket item over time through installment payments (i.e., "I can't pay for this all today, but I can pay it back little by little over a few months").

- INTEREST RATES: Watch out for interest rates when buying something on a layaway payment plan. Low-interest or 0 percent financing offers can be enticing, but always read the fine print to understand the terms and avoid hidden interest charges further down the line.

WHEN IT'S TIME TO CONSIDER A LOAN

- BIG PURCHASES: Loans can be convenient for big-ticket purchases like a car, home, or study fees. (Whereas layaway lets you receive your item(s) and allows you to pay in full over time, loans just give you the money and let you pay it back over time.)

- EMERGENCIES: When disaster strikes, a loan can provide a lifeline to cover urgent expenses like medical bills or home repairs. Just be sure to explore all your options and choose the best loan terms for your situation.

TIPS FOR SAFE BORROWING

- RESEARCH LENDERS: Make sure you stay well away from loan sharks and predatory lenders by researching reputable financial institutions or online lenders with positive (and authentic) customer reviews and transparent terms.

- READ THE FINE PRINT: Don't sign on the dotted line until you've read and understood all the terms and conditions. Look out for hidden fees, high interest rates, or prepayment penalties that could come back to haunt you.

- BORROW RESPONSIBLY: Only borrow what you can afford to repay comfortably. Assess your budget to choose a loan amount and repayment schedule that fits within your means.

Overdrafts

An overdraft is essentially a safety net for your bank account. If you accidentally overspend, your overdraft is there as a temporary lifeline to cushion your fall and cover you until you can replenish your funds and get back on your feet. But beware—overdrafts come with their own hidden dangers, and becoming too reliant on them can be a slippery slope.

BREAKING DOWN OVERDRAFTS

An overdraft is a financial backup provided by your bank that allows you to withdraw more money than you have in your account, up to a preset limit. It's a short-term solution to a temporary cash flow problem, and you shouldn't rely on it as a long-term financial strategy.

THE PROS OF OVERDRAFTS	THE CONS OF OVERDRAFTS
CONVENIENCE: They provide immediate access to extra funds when you need them most, without the hassle of applying for a loan or credit card.	**FEES AND CHARGES:** Banks often charge hefty fees for overdraft usage, including overdraft fees and daily overdraft interest rates, which can add up quickly.
EMERGENCY BACKUP: They serve as a safety net for unexpected expenses or emergencies, giving you peace of mind knowing you have a financial cushion to fall back on if needed.	**RISK OF DEBT:** Relying too heavily on overdrafts can lead to a cycle of debt, as you pick up bad borrowing habits and find yourself up to your neck in overdraft fees.
NO CREDIT IMPACT: Unlike credit cards or loans, overdrafts typically do not impact your credit score, making them a viable option for those with less-than-perfect credit.	**LIMITED AVAILABILITY:** Overdraft limits vary depending on your bank and account history, so you may not always be able to guarantee the funds will be there in an emergency.

THREE STEPS TO RESPONSIBLE OVERDRAFT USE

1. WATCH YOUR BALANCE: Keep a close eye on your account balance and avoid overdrawing your account whenever possible. Set up automatic low-balance alerts via your mobile banking apps to warn you when your funds are running low.

2. USE IT SPARINGLY: Reserve overdrafts only for true emergencies or unexpected expenses. Don't let yourself slide into bad habits.

3. KNOW YOUR LIMITS: Make sure you're all over the terms and limits of your overdraft facility to avoid the sting of unnecessary fees.

Emergency funds

We've already talked a little bit about emergency funds (as well as "f*** off" funds, the maverick cousin of the emergency fund), but now let's delve a little deeper into exactly what they are, why you might need one and how you can get started on building yours.

WHY DO YOU NEED AN EMERGENCY FUND?

- UNEXPECTED EXPENSES: From a less-than-welcome tax bill to a pricey visit to the vet, life is full of surprises, and they're not always cake.

- JOB LOSS OR INCOME REDUCTION: In today's uncertain economy, job loss or income reduction can come knocking when you least expect it (and when you're least prepared).

- HOME OR CAR REPAIRS: From a leaky roof to a broken-down vehicle, home and car repairs can be sudden and costly.

- DENTAL/MEDICAL EMERGENCIES: Health issues can arise at any time, and the last thing you want to be worrying about is how you're going to pay for medical bills or treatment.

- TRAVEL OR FAMILY EMERGENCIES: Whether it's a last-minute trip to visit a sick family member or a surprise bachelor weekend, having an emergency fund ensures you can focus on your loved ones without stressing about the cost.

HOW TO BUILD YOUR EMERGENCY FUND

- SET CLEAR SAVINGS GOALS: Calculate how much you want to save in your emergency fund, whether it's three to six months' worth of living expenses or a specific amount (i.e. "I need to have at least enough to cover a last-minute flight to see my family").

- AUTOMATE YOUR SAVINGS: Set up automatic transfers from your checking account to your emergency fund each month to help you reach your goal in no time (and without even thinking about it!).

- PRIORITIZE SAVING: Don't be tempted to skim off the top of your emergency fund for splurges or non-emergency purchases. Treat your emergency fund as a non-negotiable expense and prioritize it just as much as your other financial goals.

- REPLENISH AFTER USE: If you do have to dip into your emergency fund (for an actual emergency), make sure you replenish the funds as soon as possible to maintain your financial safety net.

"Prepare for the worst, hope for the best."

Working smarter (not harder) with passive income

Imagine making money without having to clock in everyday. Sound too good to be true? Not if you've mastered the art of passive income! If you like the idea of making money with less effort, then listen closely as we explore the world of passive income.

WHAT IS PASSIVE INCOME?

Basically, passive income is money earned with minimal effort or ongoing work—sounds like heaven, right? Instead of trading your time for money like in a traditional job, passive income streams continue to generate revenue even when you're not actively working (like, for example, when you're sleeping, traveling the world, or watching Netflix).

EXAMPLES OF PASSIVE INCOME STREAMS

- **INVESTING IN STOCKS:** Just like you learned about on pages 58–59!
- **RENTAL PROPERTIES:** Owning property and renting it out can provide a nice, steady stream of passive income.
- **DIGITAL PRODUCTS:** If you're a savvy creative type, making and selling digital products like eBooks, printables, or stock photography can generate a tidy passive income.
- **AFFILIATE MARKETING:** This is all about partnering with companies to promote their products or services through affiliate links on your website or social media and pocketing the commission (#tipsforclicks!).
- **ROYALTIES:** If you have a creative talent like writing, music, or illustration, you could earn royalties from your work over time.
- **REAL ESTATE CROWDFUNDING:** These platforms allow you to pool your funds with other investors to finance real estate projects and earn returns.
- **YOUTUBE:** Create and monetize a YouTube channel with ads or sponsored content and watch the money roll in as your views go up.

HOW TO GET STARTED GENERATING PASSIVE INCOME

- **FIGURE OUT YOUR NICHE:** Take some time to brainstorm your strengths, interests, and skills to work out the best passive income opportunities for you.
- **START SMALL:** Begin with one or two passive income streams and gradually expand as you gain experience and confidence.
- **STAY CONSISTENT:** Building passive income takes time and effort. Stick with it and don't be put off if it takes time to get it off the ground.
- **MONITOR AND ADJUST:** Regularly review your passive income streams to see what's making the most money and concentrate your efforts on your biggest earners.

Looking at the big picture

As you move into your adult life, for the first time, you might be in a position to indulge in all the things you've ever wanted. And—even better news—you've worked out you can afford to buy them! But cool your jets. Just because you can afford the upfront cost of your heart's desires, doesn't mean you can always afford it in the long-term. Sorry to be a buzzkill, but it's time to look at the big picture of big-ticket purchases.

PURCHASES WITH HIDDEN ONGOING COSTS

* PETS: If you've been scrolling through pet adoption websites, counting down the days until you can finally bring home the furry companion of your dreams, this may come as an unwelcome reality check. Pets are one of the biggest sources of hidden ongoing costs of any purchase you can make. From vet bills and food to toys and grooming, being a pet parent comes with hefty (and often unpredictable) costs that can add up faster than you can say "fetch!"

> The average yearly cost of owning a dog can easily run into the thousands.

* CARS: Pulling up closely behind pets is cars. When you go to purchase your next ride, look beyond the sticker price and consider the costs of insurance, maintenance and fuel.

* HOUSING: When you're looking for a new place, remember that beyond the initial costs of the rent or mortgage payments, you need to be fully prepared to handle the additional, ongoing, or unexpected financial responsibilities that go hand in hand with housing. This can include the costs of furnishing the place (more expensive than you realize), keeping up with your utilities, and tackling any sudden damages or repairs.

HOW TO ACCOUNT FOR ONGOING COSTS

* DO YOUR HOMEWORK: Thoroughly research the ongoing costs associated with your purchase. Search online and ask other people in your position for their honest advice.

* LONG-TERM BUDGETING: Take a good look at your finances and be honest with yourself about whether you can afford to budget for the purchase in the long term.

* PLAN FOR THE UNEXPECTED: Life is full of surprises, so make sure you have some wiggle room in your budget for unexpected expenses that may arise.

* DECIDE WITH YOUR HEAD, NOT YOUR HEART: As hard as it might be, you need to make a sensible decision that will benefit your life in the long run, and not turn your once-joyful purchase into a source of financial stress and regret.

* CONSIDER ALTERNATIVES: Sometimes, there are more budget-friendly alternatives that can still bring joy and fulfillment into your life. Keep an open mind and explore your options.

Spending habits and tips

Okay, let's take a minute to process everything we've learned so far. It's easy to get overwhelmed with all the advice around how to manage your money, and there's only so much our soft, squishy brains can handle. What's that you say? What you really need is some short, snappy, easy-to-remember golden rules of spending? Well, isn't this your lucky day.

THE GOLDEN RULES OF SPENDING

1. **BUDGET WISELY:** Create a budget that aligns with your financial goals and stick to it. Track your expenses and prioritize essential items over non-essentials.

2. **AVOID IMPULSE PURCHASES:** Pause before making a purchase and ask yourself if it's something you truly need or just a fleeting desire. Sleep on it, and if you still want it tomorrow, then consider buying it.

3. **LIVE BELOW YOUR MEANS:** Spend less than you earn and save the difference. Avoid lifestyle inflation and resist the temptation to keep up with fleeting trends.

4. **QUALITY OVER QUANTITY:** Invest in quality items that will last longer, even if they come with a higher price tag. It's better to buy one high-quality item than multiple cheap ones that need frequent replacement.

5. **COMPARISON SHOP:** Research prices and shop around before you buy to ensure you're getting the best value for your money. Use price-comparison websites and apps to find the best deals.

6. **DELAY GRATIFICATION:** Practice delayed gratification by postponing non-essential purchases until you can afford them without compromising your financial goals.

7. **SET SPENDING LIMITS:** Establish spending limits for different categories of expenses, such as dining out, entertainment, and clothing. Stick to these limits to avoid overspending.

8. **CASH VS. CREDIT:** Use cash for discretionary spending to avoid overspending and accumulating debt. Reserve credit cards for emergencies or planned purchases that you can pay off in full each month.

9. **SPEND ON WHAT MATTERS, SAVE ON WHAT DOESN'T:** For example, when you're grocery shopping, you could splurge on that expensive brand of oat milk you like and then opt for the supermarket own-brand tinned goods (which are usually just as good as the expensive branded stuff!).

10. **PRACTICE GRATITUDE:** Cultivate a mindset of gratitude and appreciate what you have rather than constantly seeking more. Focus on experiences and relationships over material possessions.

"If you can't buy it twice, you can't afford it."

Dealing with financial hardships

Financial hardships are a reality for many of us, but they don't have to define who you are and what your future will be. By facing challenges head-on, staying resilient, and—most importantly—knowing where to seek support when needed, we can overcome these tough times and emerge stronger than ever.

ADVICE FOR NAVIGATING ROUGH FINANCIAL SEAS

- STAY POSITIVE: Yes, it's easier said than done, but maintaining a positive outlook and reminding yourself that tough times are only temporary will allow you to focus on solutions rather than dwelling on problems.

- ASSESS YOUR SITUATION: Take an objective look at your financial situation and identify areas where you can cut back on expenses. Create a budget and prioritize essential expenses such as housing, food, and utilities.

- COMMUNICATE WITH YOUR CREDITORS: If you're having trouble paying bills or meeting financial obligations, contact your creditors as soon as possible and explain your situation. Many creditors will be willing to work with you to develop a repayment plan or offer temporary relief options.

- BUILD A SUPPORT NETWORK: Lean on your family and friends for emotional support during difficult times, and surround yourself with positive influences who can offer encouragement and guidance.

- SEEK SUPPORT: There are many resources available to assist you during tough times, so don't be afraid to reach out for help if you're struggling to make ends meet.

WHERE TO FIND HELP

- GOVERNMENT ASSISTANCE PROGRAMS: Contact your local government or visit their website to learn about available assistance programs, such as unemployment benefits, housing assistance, and food assistance programs.

- NON-PROFIT ORGANIZATIONS: Many non-profit organizations offer financial assistance, counseling services, and educational resources to help individuals facing financial hardships. Search online or reach out to your local community for recommendations.

- CREDIT OR DEBT COUNSELING AGENCIES: Reach out to reputable credit or debt counseling agencies for assistance with debt management, budgeting, and financial education. These agencies can provide personalized guidance to help you find your way through your financial situation.

Achieving financial freedom

Financial freedom isn't just about having an overflowing bank account, it's about having ultimate control over your finances and being able to live the life you want on your own terms without worrying about money. It's basically your money endgame. Let's look at the benefits of achieving financial freedom (in case you needed any more motivation) and explore the steps you can start taking today to achieve financial freedom for the rest of your life.

WHEN YOU'VE GOT FINANCIAL FREEDOM, YOU'VE GOT . . .

- **PEACE OF MIND:** Just imagine the sense of calm you'd have knowing that your financial future is secure and you can weather any unexpected challenges that come your way. Ultimate zen.

- **FREEDOM TO PURSUE YOUR PASSIONS:** The world is your oyster, and you can explore whatever passions, interests, and flights of fancy you want without being tied to the daily grind.

- **MORE TIME FOR YOUR FAMILY AND FRIENDS:** When you're not worried about your financial obligations, you can spend your time with the people you love most, nurturing your relationships and making memories to last a lifetime.

- **MORE OPPORTUNITIES TO GIVE BACK:** One of the joys of financial freedom is that it allows you to give back to your loved ones and community and support causes that are important to you, whether through charitable donations or volunteering your time and skills.

YOUR STEP-BY-STEP GUIDE TO ACHIEVING FINANCIAL FREEDOM

Along with the stellar advice on the previous pages (clearing debts, creating an emergency fund, saving, and investing), follow the tips below to help you achieve glorious financial freedom.

- **CREATE MULTIPLE INCOME STREAMS:** Diversify your income sources to reduce reliance on a single source of income. Explore opportunities for additional income streams, such as freelancing, rental properties, or passive income streams like dividends from investments.

- **LIVE BELOW YOUR MEANS:** Practice mindful spending and live below your means to maximize savings and investment opportunities. Prioritize needs over wants and avoid lifestyle inflation, even as your income increases.

- **SET CLEAR FINANCIAL GOALS:** Define your financial goals and create a roadmap for achieving them. Whether it's retiring early, starting a business, or buying a home, having clear objectives will help keep you motivated.

- **NEVER STOP LEARNING:** Invest in your financial education by reading books, attending workshops, and staying informed about personal finance topics. The more knowledgeable you are about money management and investment strategies, the better equipped you'll be to achieve financial freedom.

- **MONITOR AND ADJUST:** Regularly review your financial progress and adjust your strategies as needed. Track your income, expenses, and investment performance to ensure you're staying on track toward your goals.

- **SIT BACK AND ENJOY:** Once you've achieved financial freedom, enjoy it! You've worked hard for this, so spend time pursuing your passions, traveling, and giving back to your community. Just remember to stick to your good habits and stay disciplined so that you can enjoy your newfound freedom for the long-term.

"The best thing money can buy is financial freedom."

ROGER BERGER

P is for pensions

Picture this: you're lounging on a tropical beach, drinking out of a coconut, warming your toes on the sand, and living your best retired life, all thoughts of your working years far behind you. Sounds pretty amazing, right? Well, that dreamy retirement won't fund itself! It's time to start growing that nest egg so you can live out your golden years in comfort and style.

DIFFERENT TYPES OF PENSIONS

WORKPLACE PENSION: This is like the VIP section of pensions. Your employer sets it up, and sometimes they'll even throw in some extra cash (aka employer contributions) to sweeten the deal. Free money? Yes, please!

PRIVATE PENSION: Think of this as your personal pension plan. You set it up yourself and make regular contributions to watch it grow. And guess what—you can have a private pension even if you've got a workplace pension (because the only thing better than one nest egg, is two!).

RETIREMENT PLANNING IN FIVE SIMPLE STEPS

1. **START EARLY, THANK YOURSELF LATER:** The earlier you start squirreling away money into your pension, the more time it has to grow into a nice, fat retirement fund. Time is money's best friend (and money is financial freedom's best friend!). Have you started yet? What are you waiting for?

2. **MAXIMIZE THOSE CONTRIBUTIONS:** If your employer offers to match your pension contributions, jump on that gravy train! It's like getting a discount on your retirement savings—score!

3. **DIVERSIFY:** Don't put all your nest eggs in one basket. Spread your investments across different assets and play the financial field to reduce risk and increase your potential returns.

4. **TEND TO YOUR PENSION LOVINGLY:** Don't just set and forget your pension. Regularly check in on its performance and make changes as needed. It's kind of like nurturing an orchard full of real-life money trees; you might need to tweak the conditions from time to time to keep everything growing strong.

5. **DON'T TOUCH THAT POT:** Tempted to dip into your pension pot for a splurge? Think again! Early withdrawals from your pension fund can come with hefty fees and tax penalties. Keep your hands off!

Financial jargon glossary

They say money talks—and you can now talk back with this handy glossary of all that financial jargon no one ever taught you (but everyone else pretends they know about).

MONEY BUZZWORDS

- **APR (ANNUAL PERCENTAGE RATE):** The annual rate of interest charged on loans, credit cards, or other forms of credit, expressed as a percentage of the total amount borrowed.

- **CREDIT SCORE:** A number that represents your creditworthiness, based on your credit history.

- **INTEREST:** The cost of borrowing money, or the reward for saving/investing money.

- **ASSETS:** Things you own that have value, like cash, property, or investments.

- **LIABILITIES:** Debts or financial obligations you owe, like loans or credit card balances.

- **COMPOUND INTEREST:** Interest that's calculated on both the initial principal and the accumulated interest.

- **DIVERSIFICATION:** Spreading your investments across different assets to reduce risk.

- **INFLATION:** The rate at which the general level of prices for goods and services is rising.

- **ROI (RETURN ON INVESTMENT):** A measure of the profitability of an investment, usually expressed as a percentage.

- **EQUITY:** The value of ownership in an asset after all debts and liabilities have been paid off.

- **SELF-INVESTED PERSONAL PENSION (SIPP) AKA A 401(K), SUPERANNUATION, OR WORKPLACE PENSION:** A retirement savings plan sponsored by an employer, allowing employees to save and invest a portion of their paycheck before taxes.

- **IRA (INDIVIDUAL RETIREMENT ACCOUNT):** A tax-advantaged investment account for retirement savings.

- **NET WORTH:** The total value of your assets minus your liabilities, representing your overall financial health.

- **STOCKS:** Ownership shares in a corporation, entitling the owner to a share of the company's assets and profits (and losses).

- **BONDS:** Fixed-income securities representing a loan made by an investor to a borrower (typically a corporation or government).

- **CAPITAL GAINS:** Profits earned from the sale of assets such as stocks, bonds, or real estate, which are subject to taxation.

- **NET INCOME:** The amount of money left over after subtracting expenses from income, also known as profit or earnings.

- **DOWN PAYMENT:** An initial payment made toward the purchase of a large asset, such as a home or car, typically representing a percentage of the total purchase price and paid upfront at the time of the sale.

- **AMORTIZATION:** The process of paying off a debt, such as a mortgage or loan, over time through regular payments that include both principal and interest.

Health and Well-being

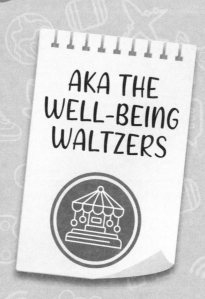

AKA THE
WELL-BEING
WALTZERS

Okay, okay. So, the Well-being Waltzers might not be the fastest, shiniest, or most thrilling ride in Adult Land, but it is without a doubt the most important. "Why's that?" I hear you ask. Because as soon as this ride breaks down, so do all the others.

As you'll see, this ride is made up of multiple cars that spin independently around a central point (spoiler alert: that's you). Each car represents a different aspect of your health and well-being, and you need to keep them all spinning for the ride to work properly. It might sound like a lot to juggle, but don't worry—there's a trick to it. Mastering the Well-being Waltzers is all about cultivating healthy habits, practicing those healthy habits consistently, and being gentle to yourself along the way.

Be your own life coach

For most people, your physical and mental health are some of the first things you really have any kind of control over, long before you get to be responsible for all that other fun stuff like jobs, rent, studying, and remembering to put the trash out. From the moment you say to yourself, "Okay, I think that's enough cheesecake for one day," or "You know what, I'm going to get an early night," you're starting to take responsibility for your health and well-being. You're prioritizing yourself. You're advocating for yourself. You're becoming your own life coach.

And this is the first step to really making progress—realizing that you are responsible for your health and well-being and taking ownership of it. You can certainly call on other people to support you on this journey, but ultimately, it's up to you.

Now, don't worry if you're not a green-smoothie-chugging wellness warrior; there's no time like the present to start getting into the right habits, routines, and mindset to prioritize your physical and mental health and set yourself up for success in all areas of your life. So, grab a healthy snack, refill your water bottle, and don't forget to stretch, because we're about to dive headfirst into all things health and well-being.

Sleeping your way to success

One of the first changes you might notice as you glide into adulthood is your relationship with sleep. As a kid, the idea of staying up past your bedtime was the ultimate act of youthful rebellion. You probably thought, "When I grow up, I'm going to stay up as late as I want!".

And then . . . you grow up. And you get a new dream. It's a dream of early nights, novelty pajamas, and high thread counts. And it's glorious. Before you know it, you're setting yourself your own bedtime (oh, if only younger you could see you now).

If you haven't already, you'll soon figure out that getting the right quantity and quality of sleep is one of the most significant contributors to your overall health and well-being. So, let's pull back the covers on all things sleep and find out how you can conquer the Land of Nod.

The A to Zzzs of sleep hygiene

A	Avoid drinking **alcohol** at least four hours before bed.
B	**Blue light** (the kind that comes from screens) is one of the biggest sleep thieves. Avoid screens for at least an hour before bed.
C	Avoid **caffeine** for at least eight hours before bed.
D	Keep your room as **dark** as possible. Artificial light—especially the blue light from screens—disrupts your body's natural rhythms.
E	Regular **exercise** helps you fall asleep more quickly and improves your sleep quality.
F	Eating fatty, sugary, or heavy **foods** before bed can cause digestion problems and make it harder for you to fall asleep.
G	Try to **get up** and **go to sleep** at the same time every day, even on the weekends.
H	**Hack** your sleep—download a sleep app to get some insights into your sleep habits (you might be surprised!).
I	**Invest** in a good quality bed, mattress, and bedding.
J	Try **journaling** before bed to clear your head and keep those sleep-stealing racing thoughts at bay.
K	A pillow between your **knees** (if you sleep on your side) or under your **knees** (if you sleep on your back) helps align your hips, spine, and pelvis and prevents lower back pain.
L	Want to **live longer**? Studies have shown that regularly getting the right quantity and quality of sleep can increase your life expectancy by up to five years.
M	Good sleep is crucial for your **mental health**—it improves your mood and reduces anxiety, stress, and depression.
N	Keep **noise** to a minimum while you're sleeping. If you struggle to sleep in silence, try listening to some ambient sounds, like rain or white noise.
O	Sleep **optimizes** your brain function and memory. While you're dozing, your brain is busy processing all the things you learned that day in a clever little process called consolidation.
P	Sleep also has incredible **physical health** benefits—from improving your immunity to lowering your risk of obesity and heart disease.
Q	Getting the right **quantity** of sleep is crucial. Aim for seven to nine hours each night (any more or less may have negative effects on your physical and mental health).
R	Get into a relaxing routine before bed. This will help signal to your brain that it's time to wind down.
S	**Sleep masks** are a great (and *très chic*) way to block out light and tell your brain it's sleep o'clock.
T	Make sure your room is at the optimum **temperature** for a peaceful sleep. Generally, you want to keep the room as cool as possible.
U	**Use** your bed only for sleep and sex. This helps your brain associate your bed with sleep.
V	Studies have shown that certain **vitamins**—in particular, vitamin D, C, and the B vitamins—can help improve your sleep.
W	Sleep can help you maintain a healthy **weight**.
X	Talk to an **expert** (yes, that's cheating, but come on, 'X' is hard). If you're struggling to get enough sleep or constantly feel tired, speak to a doctor or sleep specialist.
Y	Some gentle **yoga** stretches before bed can prepare your body and mind for a peaceful sleep.
Z	Turn your bedroom into a **zen** haven (we're talking lavender essential oils, soft lighting, whale songs . . . you get it) to create your maximum level of calm and relaxation.

Food, glorious food

Remember those days when your meals magically appeared on the table? And the cupboards were always full? Well, alas, that gravy train has left the station (that's right, you've got to make your own gravy now, too).

But there is light at the end of the gravy train tunnel. One of the joys of early adulthood is that you get to start a brand-new relationship with food. You've got a whole new world of flavors, recipes, and meal planning to explore, and while that's super exciting, it can also feel a little daunting at first. Where do you begin? What do you cook? How can you tell if those flavors will go together? Why does that milk smell so funky . . .

Luckily for you, we've broken down the fundamentals of food into some nice, bitesize, easily digestible chunks to get you cooking with gas in no time.

> Psst, while we're here...
> ## ARE YOU DRINKING ENOUGH WATER?
> Aim to drink at least eight glasses of water every day.

FOR STARTERS . . .

1. It's super important to be aware of what goes into your food, and making your own meals is the number one way to take charge of your nutrition. There are tons of recipes, blogs, and follow-along cooking videos online—it's never been easier to learn to cook for free! Give it a try—you can't eat instant noodles forever.

2. Invest in some decent cookware. You don't have to spend an arm and a leg, but you can do a bit of research to find the best basics for your price range. A good set of knives, in particular, will get you chopping and dicing your way to a Michelin Star before you know it.

> ## AIM TO EAT FIVE SERVINGS OF VEGETABLES AND TWO SERVINGS OF FRUIT EACH DAY (A SERVING IS ABOUT 80 G).

BUSTING FOOD MYTHS

MYTH: Fats and carbs are bad for you.

FACT: Fats and carbs both play an important role in a healthy diet, but not all fats and carbs are created equal. Stick to "healthy" fats (like olive oil, avocado, nuts, and oily fish) and limit your intake of "bad" fats, like butter, cheese, and ice cream. Reach for slow-release carbs like sweet potato, wholemeal bread, and brown rice over more sugary, fast-release carbs like white bread, pasta, and white rice.

MYTH: Sugar is bad for you.

FACT: There's natural sugar in a lot of things—like milk and fruit—and this kind of sugar is fine in moderation. The sugar to watch out for is added sugar—that's the kind you get in cake, soda, and chocolate. Excessive consumption of this kind of sugar is linked to a bunch of nasty health problems, like heart disease and diabetes.

MYTH: Meat is the best source of protein.

FACT: While lean meat might usually have the highest percentage of protein, that's not the end of the story. Plant proteins—like beans, legumes, nuts, quinoa, seeds, and whole grains—are also very high in protein, keep you fuller for longer and are packed with nutrients, fiber, and antioxidants.

Don't grocery shop when hungry! You'll end up buying things you don't need to satisfy your immediate hunger cravings. Make a list and stick to it—think about what you're going to cook that week and don't go rogue.

MEAL PREP IS YOUR FRIEND

1. Having to plan three meals for yourself every day takes a lot of mental load. Take the guesswork out of mealtimes by getting into good food prep habits. Sunday is a great day to do a big cook-up and prep for the week ahead (and remember to make a bit extra so you can freeze it!).

2. Win breakfast and you'll win the day. If you skip breakfast, you're more likely to reach for sugary or high-carb foods later in the day to keep you going. Prep your breakfasts the night before—overnight oats are a great, cheap, slow-release breakfast that you can prep ahead of time. Plus, the topping options are endless, so you won't get sick of them!

We like to move it, move it

There's no denying it: as you enter adulthood, your physical fitness (like pretty much everything else) takes on a new dimension. You might start to notice the occasional creak, crack, or twinge here and there, and you also might find that it takes you longer to bounce back after an injury.

Whether you're a born athlete or a snooze button in human form, this is the perfect time to prioritize your relationship with exercise. No longer should working out be an afterthought or something you do only once in a blue moon. From now on, exercise should have a regular slot in your daily schedule and before long, you're going to be reaping the benefits and wondering why you didn't start sooner. Feeling pumped? Let's do this!

THE PHYSICAL AND MENTAL BENEFITS OF EXERCISE

Think of exercise as the catalyst that sets your mood, boosts your energy, and greases the gears in your body. It's an investment in your current and future self that you will never regret. Once you start moving your body regularly, you'll enjoy a whole range of incredible physical health benefits, from weight management and improved heart health to increased concentration, better sleep quality, and clearer skin. And the effects on your mental health are just as powerful. Staying active can reduce stress, anxiety, and depression as well as boost your self-esteem, confidence, and sense of control.

So, which type of exercise is best? Ideally, a good combination of different types of exercises will help you to get the maximum benefits for your physical and mental health. Let's find out some more about each one.

> "I exercise to celebrate my body, not to punish it."

AEROBIC EXERCISE

- Aerobic exercise is any kind of exercise that gets your heart pumping and increases your need for oxygen. It strengthens your heart, lowers your blood pressure, and builds your endurance.

- Common types of aerobic exercise include running, jumping, swimming, cycling, and dancing.

- Aim for at least 150 minutes of moderate-intensity activity each week (for example, a 30-minute brisk walk or light jog five times a week).

STRENGTH TRAINING

- Strength training is any activity that uses weights or resistance to make your muscles work harder than they normally do. It increases your muscles' strength, size, power, and endurance.

- You can strength train using weights and machines at the gym, or perform bodyweight or banded movements at home (such as squats, lunges, and other push or pull movements) or at a class.

- Aim for two or three strength training sessions or classes each week.

STRETCHING

- Stretching keeps your muscles flexible, strong, and healthy. It also prepares your muscles for vigorous exercise, so remember to stretch before any workout.

- Yoga is a fantastic stretching practice that's perfect for beginners, so you'll be showing off your flex appeal in no time.

- Ideally, you should incorporate some light stretching into every day (for example, when you wake up or before you go to sleep), and schedule in more intense stretching sessions three or four times a week.

BALANCE TRAINING

- Balance training improves your muscle strength and joint support and reduces the likelihood of injuries from a fall.

- Tai chi is an amazing, gentle balance training activity that is perfect for all ages and ability levels.

- Because balance training tends to be low-intensity, you can incorporate these exercises into your daily schedule.

Body beautiful

Our bodies go through an enormous amount of upheaval in our late teens and early adulthood, and feeling confident in our changing bodies doesn't always come naturally. So, in a world that seems to whisper endless critiques, unsolicited opinions, and unrealistic expectations about what we should look like, it's time to turn up the volume on self-love.

Body positivity isn't a trend, a phase, or a blip on the cultural landscape. It's here to stay. We are tired of being bombarded with unhealthy depictions of the "ideal" body, so we're fighting back. We're breaking out of the confines of ridiculous beauty standards and embracing our incredible bodies in all their authentic glory. Breathe it in. It smells like revolution.

SOMEBODY TO LOVE

So how do we actually get better at loving our bodies? Check out these simple strategies that you can start implementing today to change your relationship with your body.

- Stick positive affirmations around your mirror.
- Get rid of your scales. Seriously. Chuck them.
- Buy clothes for the body you have now. Don't delay looking gorgeous and feeling confident until some imaginary future version of yourself is ready to shine. If your body shape changes, that's fine. Don't torture yourself in the meantime.

WHO'S THE FAIREST OF THEM ALL?

In the space below, write down five things you love about your body. They could be literally anything, for example, "I love that I have the same nose as my grandfather," "I love my fingers because without them I couldn't play the guitar," or "I love this freckle because it kind of looks like a chicken nugget." If you don't want to write them down here, that's totally fine. Pop them on a scrap of paper or in your notes on your phone. Then, go and find a mirror, stand in front of it, look yourself in the eye, and say each one out loud.

1.

2.

3.

4.

5.

Repeat this activity as often as you like and try and build it into your morning routine. Before you know it, it will come as automatically to you as remembering to brush your teeth.

Loving yourself is the greatest revolution.

Health check yourself before you wreck yourself

Like any well-oiled machine, your body needs regular check-ups to make sure everything's working in tip-top condition. As an adult, you're now entirely responsible for scheduling and attending regular health checks—even if everything feels fine. Catching any potential problems early is only ever going to be a good thing and, as tempting as it may be to never set foot inside a dentist's office again, you won't be doing yourself any favors in the long run by putting off or ignoring these routine maintenance visits. It's not glamorous, it's not sexy, but it sure is important.

Everyone has different health requirements, and if you have any pre-existing conditions then you may need certain health checks more regularly. This checklist below provides a good kick start to stay on top of the most common health checks.

DAILY AND WEEKLY

SKIN SELF-CHECK: Get into the habit of regularly checking for changes in your skin, especially if you live in a hot country or spend a lot of time in the sun. You're on the lookout for anything new, strange, or different, particularly any spots that:

- look or feel different to other spots on your skin
- have changed size, shape, color, or texture
- have sores that don't heal within a few weeks
- are itchy or bleed.

STOOL CHECKS: Yep, we're talking about poop. We all do it, and it's actually a very useful indicator of your body's overall health. Occasional changes in consistency, texture, and color are quite common and usually directly related to your diet, but if you notice consistent changes, a sudden shift in the frequency you go, or blood in your stool, get yourself a doctor ASAP.

SET UP REMINDERS ON YOUR PHONE TO KEEP ON TOP OF THE REGULAR HEALTH CHECKS YOU NEED.

MONTHLY AND ANNUALLY

- **BREAST SELF-EXAMINATION**
  If you have them, check your boobs about once a month for any changes in size, shape, or texture. Use your fingers to feel for lumps while standing with your arms down, standing with your arms raised and lying down. There are some great articles and videos online showing various techniques for how to do a thorough breast self-examination. Spend a few minutes getting familiar with what to do. Report any changes or concerns to your doctor as soon as you can.

- **TESTICLE SELF-EXAMINATION**
  If you have them, gently roll each testicle between your fingers during or after a warm shower to check for any unusual lumps, swelling, or changes in size or shape. Try and do this about once a month and be sure to report any concerns to a doctor right away.

- **TEETH**
  Find yourself a nice dentist and go visit them every six months to a year. Getting a regular dental check-up and cleaning (along with good daily dental hygiene) will help prevent any nasty issues from forming in the first place. Now that's something to smile about.

- **SEXUAL HEALTH CHECK**
  If you're sexually active, you should also get a full sexual health check once a year or every three to six months if you have multiple partners.

LONG-TERM

- It's a good idea to book in an eye test every two years (if you haven't already been identified as being at risk of eye diseases, in which case you may need to go more frequently).

- If you're between the ages of 21–65 and you have a cervix, make sure you schedule a cervical screening (also known as a pap test) every three years. Depending on where you live, you may receive a letter from the government reminding you that you're due for a pap test, but if you don't receive a letter, you should still schedule an appointment with your GP.

- If you're under 45 and in good health, you should book in to visit your GP for a general check-up every couple of years, even if you feel fine. The doctor will take a look at things like your heartbeat, blood pressure, height, and weight, and review the state of your overall health.

THE MIND-BODY CONNECTION

Being a good caretaker and advocate for your body not only benefits your physical health but also does wonders for your mental health. When your body feels good, your mind often follows suit, releasing feel-good hormones, reducing stress, and boosting your mood. Investing your time and energy into your physical health is a powerful demonstration of self-respect, self-confidence, and self-love.

Love thy selfie

Self-love has become a bit of a buzzword of late, and you'll often see it thrown around by advertisers or influencers pretty casually. A quick search for #selflove on Instagram will turn up a never-ending feed of well-staged photos of steaming tea, cozy blankets, and bubble baths. While these are all great expressions of self-love, they don't exactly give you an idea of how you go about building it. The good news is that self-love is a skill you can learn like any other. It takes time, patience, and inner work, but it's so worth it and the effects will ripple through every part of your life.

WHAT EXACTLY IS SELF-LOVE?

Self-love means having a strong sense of respect, affinity, and compassion for yourself. When you have self-love, you recognize your own worth and treat yourself lovingly—this includes the way you speak to and about yourself (more on this later).

It's important to note that self-love is not the same as narcissism, which is characterized by an exaggerated sense of self-importance, an excessive need for admiration, and staggering self-absorption (you've got someone in mind, haven't you?). Generally speaking, narcissism is associated with poor mental health and a lack of empathy for others, whereas self-love has an overwhelmingly positive effect on your mental well-being and relationships with others.

BENEFITS OF SELF-LOVE

1. LOWER STRESS, INCREASED RESILIENCE
   The root cause of stress is often feelings of inadequacy—basically, a situation crops up and we don't feel capable of handling it, which creates feelings of stress. When you have a well-established sense of self-love, you feel confident in your ability to take on challenging situations, thus reducing your feelings of stress and making you more resilient in the face of life's challenges.

2. TAKE RISKS
   Having a strong sense of self-love drives us to take risks and try new things. It gives us faith that not only will we be able to deal with an outcome if it doesn't go to plan, but that we're worth the risk to find out. Self-love drives us forward out of love, not fear. It's what motivates us to take chances and strive for success.

3. EMPATHY
   When we truly embrace our authentic selves with compassion, understanding, and appreciation, it increases our empathy toward ourselves and others. Self-love inspires us to take care of our physical and mental health and protects us from negative or intrusive thoughts, self-sabotage, and burning out. In short, it makes us kinder.

SELF-LOVE STARTER KIT

So now we know the "why" of self-love, let's get down to the "how."

- **PRACTICE MINDFULNESS AND MEDITATION**
  These are powerful tools to help you calm your mind, declutter your headspace, and recenter yourself.

- **PRACTICE SPEAKING KINDLY TO YOURSELF**
  This one is so important. Your inner voice is the voice you'll hear most in your life. Think about that for a moment. If you wouldn't say it to someone you love, don't say it to yourself.

- **GET BETTER AT ACCEPTING COMPLIMENTS**
  Try the activity from page 82 but include all the things you love about yourself, not just your body.

- **SET BOUNDARIES**
  This is a big one but a tough one. Self-love means respecting yourself enough to create firm boundaries over who and what has access to your time and energy. This also feeds into . . .

- **SAYING NO**
  Be prepared to say no to the things you don't want to do, you don't have the time to do, or that simply don't serve you. This is all part of creating boundaries and loving yourself enough to dedicate your time and energy to the things that serve you.

- **SAYING YES**
  Okay, slightly self-contradictory, but this is about opening yourself up to new experiences and having the courage and self-belief to try new things.

Your self-love journey will look different to everyone else's, but these simple strategies are a great place to start. Remember, your first love affair should be with yourself.

Bye-bye, bad vibes

Have you ever felt like you have a dark, gloomy cloud following you around, obscuring your thoughts, weighing you down, and dampening your spirits? This can be what toxic energy feels like. Toxic energy can come from external sources—such as prolonged exposure to negative, energy-zapping people, or environments—as well as internal sources, such as your own psyche.

Whether internal or external, the impact of toxic energy can be profound. Toxic energy weakens our mental health and prevents us from moving forward with our lives. It saps our motivation and fills us with feelings of self-doubt, inadequacy, and indecision. These thoughts often race around our heads, making us distracted and unproductive while disrupting our sleeping patterns (and we all know how important sleep is by now!). This turns into a vicious cycle, where our sleep-deprived, disordered, jittery brains begin to generate more negative thoughts and feed the toxic energy. So how do we recognize when we're in a toxic energy spiral and guide ourselves out of it?

HOW TO BANISH TOXIC ENERGY

MEDITATION

There's a reason meditation crops up so often when we're talking about mental health and well-being. Meditation has a profoundly calming and healing effect on the mind and body. It relaxes your muscles, reduces your blood pressure and heartbeat, and regulates your stress hormones. It's kind of like hitting the reset button when you can't stop overthinking or when your anxious thoughts are running out of control. The stillness of meditation trains your brain to witness your thoughts rather than being overwhelmed by them, allowing you to stop toxic thoughts in their tracks before they take root.

HOW TO MEDITATE EFFECTIVELY

1. Find a quiet space where you won't be disturbed.

2. Get comfortable. Ideally, you want to be sitting with your back straight, your arms loose at your sides, and your muscles as relaxed as possible.

3. When you first start meditating, your mind will wander. This is completely normal. When the thoughts wander in, don't try to ignore them; acknowledge them, and then bring your attention back to your breath.

4. Start small. Don't try to be a zen master from the first session. Start with a short, guided meditation for beginners and build up from there. There are lots of free resources available online to help you get started.

GET OUT INTO NATURE AND EXERCISE

Spending time in nature has been proven to have a positive effect on a range of mental health issues, such as anxiety and depression. There's a reason all those sickly Victorian ladies were sent to take the air by the sea in the 19th century (why don't we still do that?). Being among nature promotes feelings of calmness, clarity, and connection. While you're out there, get your heart rate up and bring your cortisol (stress hormone) levels down with a bit of exercise. As well as the numerous other physical and mental health benefits of exercise, a brief jog around the block could help stop those negative thoughts from catching up with you. Yes, sometimes you *can* run away from your problems.

And speaking of nature, if you have a pet (or can borrow one), multiple studies have shown that spending time cuddling with a furry friend can also significantly boost your mental health by increasing your levels of dopamine, serotonin, and oxytocin (let's just call them the "happy hormones"). As if we needed another excuse to snuggle a puppy.

DO SOMETHING FOR SOMEONE ELSE

Often, when we're in a negative thought spiral, we become so absorbed by what we're struggling with that we lose perspective and allow it to become a monster in our heads. Shifting our focus to serving another person can be a powerful way to recalibrate our thinking and gain a little perspective into the reality of our challenges. Volunteering to help a friend, family member, or even a stranger can produce significant feelings of connection and belonging—two feelings that often get lost in the cloud of toxic energy, which feeds on isolation.

Coping with trauma

Trauma can enter our lives at any time, wearing any number of different guises. It can come in the form of sudden, unexpected events—like accidents, natural disasters or crime—or long-term, ongoing stressors, such as illness, poverty, and abuse.

DID YOU KNOW?
You can also experience trauma from things that don't happen directly to you. Prolonged exposure to information about traumatic events (yes, even doom-scrolling) or proximity to victims of trauma can affect you in the same way as first-hand trauma. This is called vicarious trauma, and it's just as valid as first-hand trauma.

TOOLS FOR TRAUMA
As young children, those who care about us often try to shield us from suffering out of love and concern for our well-being. However, as we enter adulthood, this can leave us feeling unprepared to process not only our own trauma but that of those around us and the world at large. So, how can we protect ourselves in the face of trauma?

TALK TO SOMEONE: This is at the top of the list for a reason. Whether it's a trusted friend, a family member or a trained therapist, it's so important to reach out and connect with someone to talk through your feelings.

LET YOURSELF FEEL YOUR FEELNGS: After a traumatic event or in the face of ongoing trauma, your instinct might be to try to push down your emotions to try and block out the pain. This will only delay your recovery. Give yourself the time and space to work through your emotions at your own pace.

LOOK AFTER YOURSELF PHYSICALLY: Continue to eat well and get lots of sleep, and exercise. Avoid turning to alcohol or drugs—substances that numb your feelings can seem like a tempting coping mechanism, but this will only make you feel worse in the long run.

Remember, trauma looks different for everyone, and your journey to recovery will be unique. The steps above are a good foundation to build upon as you discover exactly what you need to heal.

It's okay to not be okay.

It's okay to ask for help.

It's okay to need time.

Healthy hobbies

In the whirlwind of all our fun new adult responsibilities, it's very easy to get sucked into the work-eat-sleep cycle and forget to make time for ourselves. As a kid, there seemed to be infinite time for our hobbies. Games, sports, art, dance, theater, music . . . we were encouraged to try them all! "Do I want to try jiu-jitsu? Sure!", "Would I like to learn the flute? Why not?" Many of us discover our passions as children, and then as soon as we grow up, suddenly there's no time to do any of them. What a shame.

But no more! In a world where busyness reigns supreme, hobbies offer a refuge, allowing us to reconnect with our passions, dreams, and personal identities. They're gateways to self-discovery and self-care; they're the canvas where creativity thrives. Embracing our hobbies isn't just about finding an escape; it's a vital pursuit to rediscover who we are at our core, reclaim lost joy, and create space for our mental and emotional needs amidst life's hustle and bustle.

SOCIAL HOBBIES

Social hobbies are hobbies that you do with other people—but they're so much more than that. From book clubs and sports teams to group art sessions or volunteering, social hobbies weave a tapestry of social bonds, shared experiences, and mutual support, allowing you to create a network of like-minded friendships and a sense of belonging. Whether you're into bingo, basketball, or bird-watching, there are bound to be others out there just waiting to share their passions with you too. Search online for local hobby groups you might want to try out or, if there's nothing that tickles your fancy, start your own group!

SOLO HOBBIES

As the name suggests, solo hobbies are those enriching activities that you do by yourself. Whether it's reading, painting, hiking, or playing a musical instrument, these hobbies serve as portals to inner reflection and introspection. They offer moments of calmness and serenity, and act as sanctuaries for self-expression and exploration without external pressures. Investing time in solo hobbies is an important part of building self-love, as you find joy in your creativity, independence, and self-reliance. Whether you already have a solo hobby or you're keen to give one a try, carve out some regular time in your schedule and treat this as sacred "you time," not to be rescheduled or shuffled to make room for work or other commitments.

COPING WITH LONELINESS

It's one of the great paradoxes of our time: we've never been more connected and we've also never been more disconnected. Despite having more ways than ever to reach out to each other, it can sometimes feel impossible to cut through the noise and find genuine connection. Loneliness is a real modern-day epidemic, and people who suffer from loneliness experience physical symptoms such as increased stress and inflamation and lower immunity.

There's no doubt about it, making friends as an adult can be tough, especially if you're moving away from your long-established networks in your home or college town. But, by trying a few simple techniques, you can take the first steps to combat loneliness and build meaningful relationships to last:

- Make the first move. Don't sit around waiting for the phone to ring—reach out to your existing network. Even if it's been a long time since you spoke to someone, try reigniting your old connections.

- Be vulnerable. This one is easier said than done, but if you don't put yourself out there, you'll limit your opportunities to meet amazing new people who could become lifelong friends.

- Join clubs or groups. Try mixing in some social hobbies with your solo pursuits. Joining a running club or group exercise class is a great way to meet people in a less intense scenario—you're doing a shared activity together so you don't need to scramble to make conversation.

- Do the things you love and you'll meet other people who love those things too. There's no better way to meet like-minded people.

Navigating bad days

Occasionally, that cloud of toxic energy can become so dense and heavy that it turns into a full-on storm. When that happens, even the simplest tasks can feel overwhelming, and it can be hard to see a way out. It's important to realize that we all have days like this sometimes, and your feelings are completely valid. This section isn't about trying to avoid those days (we've already covered that in the previous sections about building self-love and banishing toxic energy), it's about how to best get yourself through it when the storm clouds arrive.

> **While the occasional bad mental health day is normal, if you are struggling with a prolonged period of feeling depressed, anxious, or emotionally disconnected, reach out to a mental health professional who can work with you to come up with a long-term treatment plan.**

BAD DAY SURVIVAL TIPS

1. **DON'T FORGET BASIC SELF-CARE**
   During bad mental health days, it's important to still take care of your basic hygiene and self-care. To be clear, we're not talking about face masks, mani-pedis, and bath bombs here. This is your bread-and-butter wash-your-face-and-clean-your-teeth kind of self-care. These small acts, like making your bed, taking a shower, and putting on clean clothes, will not only increase your feelings of self-worth but will generate feelings of accomplishment that will slowly contribute to positive feelings.

2. DON'T FORGET TO EAT AND DRINK

Reduced appetite is a common symptom of depression so, on bad days, you may not feel like eating much at all. It's fine to keep your meals small and simple, but it's crucial that you eat something to regulate your blood sugar and give you the physical and emotional energy to make it through the day. Keep sipping water throughout the day, too, as dehydration can contribute to headaches and brain fog.

3. DON'T TRY TO DO TOO MUCH

Depending on your personal circumstances, you may still have to work, study, or care for others during a bad mental health episode. Keep your responsibilities to a bare minimum when possible, delegate tasks to others if you can, and be firm with your boundaries around what's achievable for you. Nothing is more important than your health, so do what you can and be gentle with yourself.

4. LEAN ON YOUR COMFORTS

Ideally, on bad mental health days, you can have some time to relax and recover. If that's the case, now's the time to go big on comfort. Get your cuddliest blanket, throw on your favorite cheesy movie, and maybe indulge in some of your comfort foods. Finding joy in the little things is crucial and can even alleviate some of the heaviness of mental health challenges. Watching your favorite movie or TV show will act as a distraction, a mood booster, and provide a sense of calm and control (as you already know what's going to happen).

5. PUT YOUR PHONE AWAY

If you need to be contactable for work or family emergencies, you may not be able to shun your phone entirely but try to limit the amount of time you spend scrolling on social media or news sites. The news is often confronting and anxiety-inducing and social media is full of falsified, idealized projections of other people's lives that may send you into a comparison spiral. Unplugging for a day (or at least a few hours) might just be the ticket to some much-needed mental peace.

6. GET SOME FRESH AIR AND SUNSHINE

When you're going through a difficult time, it can be tempting to draw the curtains, pull the comforter over your head and try to block the world out. If you're feeling up to it, try going for a gentle walk, or just sitting outside and letting the sun warm your face. Sunlight is a well-known mood booster and simply getting out of the house and into a new environment will force your brain to form new connections, which is a fantastic way of getting yourself out of a rut when you have racing thoughts.

MY AFFIRMATIONS

When you're feeling up to it, fill this section with affirmations and mantras that you think will speak to you when you're experiencing a bad mental health episode. We've given you one to get you started, but ultimately, your own words will resonate the most with you.

1. **All storms run out of rain.**

2.

3.

4.

5.

Dating and Relationships

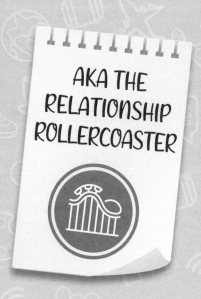

AKA THE
RELATIONSHIP
ROLLERCOASTER

Love is in the air

Dating as a modern-day adult can be exciting, confusing, exhilarating, and devastating—sometimes all at once. You're trying to find someone you connect with and who's on your wavelength while still trying to figure out who you are and what your wavelength even is.

Or, perhaps you've already found your person but you're struggling to juggle the changes and demands that adulthood involves within your relationship?

As you venture into the dating world, you'll no doubt be bombarded with well-intentioned but conflicting advice from friends and family, dating trends that come and go quicker than you can say "zombieing," and just *so many apps*.

Sit tight, because we're going to debunk some dating myths, unpack some dating dos and don'ts, and generally demystify dating in the modern era.

Connections old and new

At this point in your life, you'll probably notice that it's not just your romantic relationships that are becoming more layered. Your relationship with your family members might take on a new dynamic, especially if you're living away from home for the first time. If you move away for work or study, you'll also probably experience some disruption to the rhythm of your now long-distance friendships, which can be unsettling.

And then there are the new relationships you'll welcome into your life. If you're starting a new job, heading to college, or moving to a new city, there's a good chance you'll be meeting lots of different people from lots of different backgrounds. You might even be discovering completely new types of relationships, for example, having colleagues and housemates for the very first time.

This section will give you helpful tips, advice, and strategies to communicate effectively, build stronger bonds, and find fulfillment in your relationships, both old and new.

Demystifying dating

First things first, let's make sure we're all clear about exactly what dating is, which is to say, it's not really one exact thing at all (helpful, right?). Basically, dating is spending time with someone you like and care about, and maybe/definitely/don't-ask-me-I-haven't-decided-yet but possibly want to pursue romantically. That's it. A lot of us tend to overthink it, but really, dating can take any form you want—as long as everyone is on the same page (crucial).

WHAT ARE YOU LOOKING FOR?

No matter how you go about it, it's important to have a clear idea of what you want out of dating before you start. Looking for a fling? Have at it. In it for the long haul? Love that for you. Figuring out your relationship goals? Pfft, who isn't?

The important thing is to be honest and upfront with other people (and yourself) about your dating intentions—that way, you're not wasting anyone's time or racking up any bad dating karma.

HOW DO YOU MEET SOMEONE?

Luckily, there are now more ways than ever to dip your toe in the dating pool. Try one, try them all—the dating world is your oyster.

HOW?	WHAT ARE THE UPSIDES?	WHAT ARE THE DOWNSIDES?
DATING APPS	You have *so* many choices and can test the waters with a little conversation before you meet up.	They also have *so* many choices, so can be quick to judge and may have short attention spans.
BLIND DATE/SET-UP	They've already been vetted by someone who knows you and thinks you'll hit it off.	The person who set you up might be a bit too invested in the relationship.
SPEED DATING	You can practice the art of conversation in a low-stakes environment and meet *loads* of eligible singles.	You'll have to make a lot of small talk and probably cover the same topics over and over . . .
REAL-LIFE (SO RETRO)	You'll feel like you're living out your very own *Notting Hill* love story. Adorable.	You won't know much about them at first, so you'll have to work harder to gather intel.
FRIENDS FIRST	You already know you like them and have things in common so you've got a solid foundation.	You've got to think about how it could affect the dynamics of your friendship group (especially if you break up).

Dating dos and don'ts

If you were brought up on a diet of dating shows and 90s rom-coms, you can be forgiven for thinking there are strict dating rules that everyone else seems to know. "Always wait three days before following up after a date," "Women should play hard to get," "You shouldn't kiss on the first date . . ." etc., etc., etc. *Yikes.* Luckily, game-playing and gender norms are increasingly becoming a thing of the past in dating, as our more progressive generation says *thank you, next* to restrictive rules. However, certain things just make sense when it comes to good dating etiquette, so add these timeless tips to your romance toolbox.

DO	DON'T
Think about who will pay: If you were the one who asked for the date, there's a good chance the other person is assuming you'll pay. If you'd rather split the bill, you can avoid a lot of awkwardness by bringing it up beforehand.	**Be late:** Yes, it was once considered fashionable to be late, but it was also once considered fashionable to pluck your eyebrows to death, so some things are best left in the past. Do your best to arrive on time and let your date know if you're running late.
Show interest: Ask lots of questions, make eye contact, and speak and listen with equal attention (e.g. don't just talk about yourself for the entire date, even if they are a little more reserved than you).	**Be on your phone the whole time:** Does this one even need an explanation? Put your phone away, unless you're showing your date cute vacation or pet pics.
Be yourself: Don't try to be something you're not. You want them to like you for who you really are, not a rehearsed, fake version of yourself.	**Bring up your previous relationships:** Particularly on the first date. Once you start spending more time together, the topic of previous relationships will naturally come up, but try not to dwell on them too much. Focus on the better times ahead.
Put your best foot forward: Dress up in a way that makes you feel good about yourself, and be polite and considerate (and not just to your date, but to everyone else you come across).	**Get in your head too much:** Don't overthink it—a date is just two (or more, if that's your thing) people hanging out and seeing if they hit it off. Don't put too much pressure on it. Enjoy the moment.
Follow-up: Fire off a quick message after the date to say thanks and let them know you enjoyed meeting them. If you want to see them again, great! If you didn't really gel, no worries. Just let them down gently (see page 102).	**Leave people guessing:** This is a big no-no. Ghosting (disappearing from the face of the earth) and zombieing (ghosting then mysteriously resurrecting in the DMs) wastes people's time and make you seem like a flake. Boo.

Boundaries for healthy relationships

Whether you're in a new or established relationship, one of the most important foundations of any bond—and that goes for friends and family, too—is knowing and respecting each other's boundaries. Healthy boundaries create a sense of comfort and safety and, ultimately, help you build a relationship based on trust and mutual respect.

KNOW YOUR BOUNDARIES

1. Emotional boundaries are about how you express your feelings and thoughts—including how often and how much you share—without being criticized, invalidated, or shamed.

2. Financial boundaries are about how comfortable you are talking about money, spending money, and sharing financial information with other people.

3. Intellectual boundaries are about honoring your thoughts, beliefs, ideals, and personal values when it comes to topics such as religion, politics, and science.

4. Physical boundaries include things like your need for personal space, privacy, and alone time as well as your preferences around physical touch.

5. Sexual boundaries are all about your comfort levels when it comes to sexual activity. These can change over time, so it's important to keep an open dialogue with your partner.

6. Digital boundaries are the limits you set around your phone, computer, social media accounts, and so on. This can include how comfortable you are with other people posting content about you online, how accessible you want to be online and by phone, and whether you want to share passwords with other people. Even if you trust someone completely, you should never feel pressured to share sensitive information digitally—and be particularly careful about sending explicit images or content. In the modern era, establishing and enforcing your digital boundaries is more important than ever.

DISCUSS THEM. LEARN THEM. RESPECT THEM.

ONLY "YES" MEANS "YES"

Often, when we talk about consent, we're talking about sexual consent, which is vital to be aware of, but consent also means respecting someone's boundaries in all aspects of their life. One common misconception is that consent is just about respecting when someone says "no," but it's actually a lot more than that. Consent requires a clear and emphatic "yes." Silence, uncertainty, or ambiguity does not mean "yes." Only "yes" equals consent.

Asking the big questions

So, you've found someone amazing and everything's going great. The birds are singing, the sun is shining, and you've taken to belting out love songs in the shower. All of a sudden, you find yourself daydreaming about a future with your latest squeeze. But how do you know if this relationship will pan out?

As your relationship deepens, at some point you'll need to know if you're on the same page when it comes to the big decisions in life (even ones you don't need to make just yet) before you get in too deep.

So, what kinds of questions might you need to ask each other? Depending on your personal circumstances, the list could be endless, but here are some common ones to get the ball rolling:

- Do you want kids? If so, how many kids do you imagine having?
- Do you want to get married?
- Where do you see yourself living in the future?
- Would you ever want to move overseas?
- What are your views on religion and spirituality?

RIGHT PLACE, RIGHT TIME

Yikes. Those are some big questions. You'll want to approach them very carefully, like you would a sleeping bear on a frozen lake.

First, timing is everything. You probably don't want to drop, "So, shall we open a joint bank account?" into conversation on your first date. You may find that some of these conversations come about organically, but if not, it's crucial to pick your moment. Choose a time when you're not rushed, when you have plenty of privacy, and when your partner feels relaxed.

Second, don't go into the conversation with too many assumptions or preconceived notions about how the conversation will go. No matter how well you think you know your partner, you might be surprised by their perspective on certain topics.

Third, don't expect your partner to have a well-thought-out answer in the barrel ready to go. Just because you've been thinking about it, doesn't mean they have. They might need more time to think before they answer (and this might be for the best).

Finally, remember that people can change, and the things you want (or think you want) during early adulthood may not be what you want forever. Keep an open mind and take everything into consideration before making any big decisions.

Breaking up without breaking hearts

There's no way around it, rejection sucks. Whether you're the one who got rejected or you had to turn down someone else, it can leave you feeling like a deflated balloon. Unfortunately, rejection is an inevitable part of life and relationships, but by approaching it with the right mindset, you can face all your break-ups without too many broken hearts.

DEALING WITH REJECTION

Putting yourself out there and getting rejected by someone you like can be totally devastating, but what's important is how you handle the rejection and move on. "But, how?" we hear you cry. Read on, you broken-hearted beauties.

1. REMEMBER THAT REJECTION IS NOT A REFLECTION OF YOUR SELF-WORTH: For whatever reason, this person is looking for something else in their life right now. Their decision doesn't affect your value. You know what you bring to the table. Some things just aren't meant to be, but you're just as awesome as you were yesterday.

2. BE KIND TO YOURSELF: Treat yourself, indulge yourself, spoil yourself. Turn your self-care up to 11 and send negative vibes packing while you're healing.

3. FOCUS ON THE FUTURE: Look at the rejection as a necessary plot twist in the bestselling autobiography of your life. Better times are coming, so keep your eyes on the horizon.

DOLING OUT REJECTION

If you thought getting rejected was bad, being the rejector can be even worse. It's especially hard if you care about the other person and want to protect their feelings. Here's how to let them down gently:

1. BE PREPARED, BE FIRM, BE KIND: Think carefully about what you want to say beforehand so that you can express yourself clearly and with carefully-worded compassion. Be gentle but don't leave any room for ambiguity. Making notes or talking to yourself aloud in private might help unravel the thoughts running through your head.

2. EXPRESS GRATITUDE: Tell them you're glad to have met and known them and offer them encouragement or a compliment, such as, "I know you're going to find someone amazing because that's what you deserve." Who wouldn't want to hear that?

3. DON'T GIVE FALSE HOPE: This is a tough one. It can be tempting to want to soften the blow by suggesting things might work out at some other point, but don't do it. Even if you think there could be potential in the future, it's not fair to leave people hanging. You cannot speak for your future self, so honor the way you feel right now and make it a clean break.

How to navigate a bad date

Now you're ready to date again, but this one is going . . . not so great. It happens to us all. After all, dating is a numbers game, so it's only natural that you'll have to sit through a few duds before you strike gold. Here's how to spot a bad date a mile away and make a swift escape when you find yourself stuck in one.

BEFORE THE DATE

1. Think about your red flags—maybe even jot them down in your phone—so that they're at the top of your mind and you can look out for them on the date.

COMMON RED FLAGS:

* Rude to service staff
* Plays on their phone
* Touchy-feely

* Pushy
* Complains about everything
* Interrupts/talks over you

2. When you're planning the date (especially a first date), keep it short and somewhere you can easily step away from. A quick drink, cup of coffee, or stroll around the shopping mall—ideal. A seven-course tasting menu followed by a reservation at a fancy cocktail bar which is holding a deposit on your credit card—not ideal.

3. Lay the groundwork for needing an early exit. Casually mention a big meeting the following morning, a project that needs to be finished, or a crack-of-dawn gym class. You may never need to use it, but it's worth having in your back pocket.

4. Utilize an accomplice. Ask a friend to be on standby to call you with an "emergency," if needed.

DURING THE DATE

Okay, it's officially time to declare time of death on this date. But how do you pull the plug? If your date is someone you're likely to bump into again, you might want to politely make your excuses while not burning any bridges. Or maybe the whole thing is a complete dumpster fire and you just want to get out of there as quickly as possible and never see them again. Either way, you've got options:

1. Play your excuse card (*see*, glad you laid the groundwork now, aren't you?).

2. Activate your sleeper agent. Sneak off to the bathroom and text your friend on standby to call you with the pre-planned emergency.

3. Be honest. Say, "It's been so great to meet you but I don't really feel a connection. I'm sorry. I wish you all the best."

4. If, at any point, your date makes you feel unsafe or uncomfortable, inform a member of the staff and stay with them while you wait for your ride home.

Let's talk about sex

We live in significantly more inclusive, empowered, and progressive times, especially when it comes to sex. Today, we're encouraged to explore and understand our own needs, and those of our partners, in a healthy, consensual, and non-judgmental way.

HOW TO TALK ABOUT SEX WITH YOUR PARTNER

1. Be frank. Try to avoid using euphemisms and express your wants and needs as clearly as you can. It might seem awkward or embarrassing at first, but the more you do it the easier it will be and the more fulfilling your relationships will be.

2. Be communicative. Talk often and openly about sex. Build your relationship on a foundation of communication.

3. Be understanding. When your partner expresses their wants and needs, be as understanding and empathetic as you expect them to be when you express yours.

4. Be consistent. If you've said you're not comfortable with something and your partner does it anyway, don't let it slide. Be firm and enforce your boundaries.

5. Be upfront about sexual health. Before you have sex with a new partner, it's your right to ask them if they're up to date with their sexual health checks—and be prepared to answer this question yourself, too. It's also vital to discuss birth control! Don't compromise when it comes to your health; prioritize your well-being above all else.

SAFE SEX TIPS

1. Use condoms. Even if everyone is up to date with their sexual health screenings and STD-free, it's always smart to use protection.

2. Be careful when mixing drugs and alcohol with sex. They can impair your judgment and decision-making abilities, making you more likely to engage in risky sexual behavior.

ENJOY YOURSELF

Sex is meant to be fun, so as long as you have a partner who makes you feel safe and comfortable, feel free to experiment and discover what you like and what you don't like. If you find that you're not associating sex with pleasure, comfort, and fun, you might want to reassess your sexual boundaries, needs, and desires. Seek out resources if you need further support.

What's your love language?

If you have absolutely no idea how to answer this question, then you've come to the right place. Your love language is basically how you prefer to give and receive love or affection from your friends, family, and partners. Take this quick test below to discover how you personally speak the language of lurve.

For each statement, write how strongly you agree or disagree by assigning the statement a number from 1–5:

1 = STRONGLY DISAGREE   2 = DISAGREE   3 = SORT OF   4 = AGREE   5 = STRONGLY AGREE

WORDS OF AFFIRMATION
I love it when . . .
- People tell me how much they love and appreciate me
- People thank me for doing something for them
- People encourage me and tell me they believe in me
- People say, "I love you"
- I get positive feedback

QUALITY TIME
I love it when . . .
- I spend uninterrupted quality time with my loved ones
- I can do fun and playful activities with the people I love
- My loved ones and I go on trips or explore new places
- I have deep and meaningful conversations with the people I love
- My loved ones put aside distractions and actively engage with me

GIFT-GIVING
I love it when . . .
- People mark special occasions with thoughtful gifts
- People put effort into choosing a gift for me
- People surprise me with small tokens of affection
- I find the perfect gifts for other people
- I receive thoughtful gifts

ACTS OF SERVICE
I love it when . . .
- People help me without me having to ask
- My loved ones make small gestures like making me coffee or packing my lunch for the day
- Other people take responsibility for planning and organizing
- People take tasks off my plate that they know I find difficult or boring
- My loved ones take care of practical things for me, like running errands

PHYSICAL TOUCH
I love it when . . .
- My loved ones greet me with a hug
- My loved ones touch me affectionately throughout the day
- My partner initiates physical intimacy
- People want to touch or be close to me
- My partner wants to hold hands or kiss

Now, add up your score for each section to find out which love language speaks to you most!

Maintaining adult friendships

Back on page 93, you learned that with a huge dollop of bravery, a dash of vulnerability, and a few giant leaps of faith, you can combat loneliness and make awesome friendships as an adult. But once you've found your friend group, how do you keep hold of them?

- **SCHEDULE REGULAR CHATS:** Life can get hectic, but that's no excuse to let your friendships fall by the wayside. Prioritize regular hangouts with your friends, whether it's a weekly coffee date, monthly trivia night, or an annual group getaway. Put those dates in your calendar and stick to them like glue! If your schedule really is maxed out, make sure you check in with a video chat.

- **STAY CONNECTED:** Just because you're not seeing each other in class every day anymore, doesn't mean you can't stay connected. Light up the group chat with GIFs, voice messages, and suggestions for your next chat to keep the conversation flowing.

- **GO BIG ON BIRTHDAYS:** Or any other reason to celebrate, for that matter! Make an extra effort to get together for milestones and special occasions, whether it's a new job, the new year, or National Pizza Day, jump on any excuse to get the gang together.

- **BE A GOOD LISTENER:** Just as your life is getting more complicated as you slide into adulthood, the same probably goes for your friends. Be a supportive sounding board and let your friends know, "I'll be there for you . . ." when they need to vent and hear words of encouragement and advice.

- **TRY NEW THINGS TOGETHER:** Keep old and new friendships fresh and exciting by trying new things together. Why not spend a Sunday exploring outside of your local area, check out one new restaurant a month, or take on a challenge like training for a marathon together? Whatever you choose, these shared experiences will create lasting memories and deepen your bond with your friends.

- **PRACTICE GRATITUDE:** As a kid, it's natural to take your easy childhood friendships for granted, but as you get older, you need to make sure you're actively expressing gratitude for the amazing people in your life. Get into the habit of regularly telling your friends how much they mean to you and showing them how much you appreciate their friendship through thoughtful gestures and acts of kindness.

Outgrowing your friends

As you swim further into the choppy waters of adult life, you might find that you have to leave a few people back on the shore. As hard as this is, it's also a completely natural part of growing up. Instead of fighting against the tide, if you can navigate this natural drift with grace and compassion, you'll be able to preserve the happy memories of your childhood friendships while setting yourself up for new friendships that are more aligned with the person you're becoming.

WHAT TO DO WHEN IT'S TIME TO MOVE ON

1. EMBRACE IT, DON'T FIGHT IT: Change is never easy, but if you can look at this stage of your life as a time of transformation and growth, you'll see that shedding certain parts of your life is necessary to fulfill your potential. Some people are only in your life for a season, and that's okay.

2. REFLECT ON YOUR EVOLVING PRIORITIES: As you get older, the things you value will change a lot. Get into the habit of regularly asking yourself, "Are my current friendships aligned with my values?", and "If I met these people today, would we be friends?" If not, it may be a sign that it's time to explore new connections that better resonate with who you are now.

3. DON'T FALL VICTIM TO THE SUNK-COST FALLACY: This is where you might be reluctant to abandon a long-term friendship that's no longer serving you because you've already invested so much time and energy into it. Leave the past in the past and focus on how cutting ties with this person will preserve your time and energy moving forward.

4. SEEK OUT LIKE-MINDED PEOPLE: They say you become the average of the five people you spend the most time with, so it's important to cultivate your close circle carefully. Join clubs, classes, or social groups where you can meet new friends who inspire and elevate you. Surrounding yourself with people who share your current passions and interests might give you the confidence to distance yourself from the friendships that are holding you back.

5. STAY OPEN TO RECONNECTION: While your friendships may shift and change over time, there's always the chance that you'll reconnect with old friends in the future. Don't burn your bridges and remember to stay open to the possibility of rekindling friendships down the road.

The FOMO epidemic

If you find yourself constantly refreshing your social media feeds, obsessively scrolling, and becoming increasingly distracted by your devices, you might be one of the millions of people suffering from FOMO.

Don't get us wrong, we love technology. You can book a hot vacation, a hot meal, or a hot date with the touch of a button. But having up-to-the-second updates and constant access to each other's lives means you're so focused on what everyone else is doing that the anxiety of not being part of it makes you lose interest and enjoyment in your own life. Time to get that under control.

TREAT YOUR FOMO

1. Keep a gratitude journal to focus your mind on what you have, not what you lack.

2. Do things that make you happy, even if they're not what everyone else is doing.

3. Connect with people in real life! Get outside, touch the grass, and have some authentic face-to-face interactions.

4. Do a digital detox. This is crucial if you don't want your devices to become your commanders. Start by setting Do Not Disturb hours, then get into the habit of putting your phone on airplane mode when you're spending time with people. Work your way up to a full digital detox weekend and see how good it feels to take back control of your life.

5. Embrace JOMO. "What on earth is JOMO?", we hear you cry. JOMO simply means the *joy* of missing out. It's all about the gratifying feeling of breaking away from the real or virtual activities of your social group and focusing on yourself. JOMO allows you to concentrate on what brings you peace and comfort so you can recharge your social batteries.

JOMO   FOMO

Sometimes, you have to let go of the old to make space for the new.

Found family

They say you can't choose your family. Well, we say you absolutely can. Whether you've moved far away from your relatives or you're finding that your traditional family ties are becoming increasingly strained as you find your feet in adulthood, this is the time in your life when you can choose the people who are like family to you.

WHAT DOES FOUND FAMILY MEAN?

Your found family is the group of people who might not be blood relations but who support and care for you just as much—if not more—than your actual family. The ones you call on for a no questions asked place to crash, an any time day or night ride to the airport, or a "Can you help me choose the perfect HomeGoods bedding?" weekend adventure. These people are your true-blue friends, and they'll become an even bigger part of your life as you get older.

YOUR FOUND FAMILY

Take a few minutes to jot down who is in your found family and why. If you don't have any or many found family members yet, that's okay. Instead, jot down what you're looking for in your found family.

....

....

....

....

....

....

....

....

Breaking generational curses

As you move out into the world and get a bit more distance from and perspective on your family and upbringing, you may start to find that certain habits, patterns, and traditions in your family come into a slightly different focus. We're not talking about quirks like how you always watch *Die Hard* on Christmas Eve, or the fact that your dad narrates the dog's thoughts, or that weird word for the remote control that only your family uses. We're talking about the more toxic traits that might have become normalized within your family and passed down to you. These are called generational curses.

WHAT ARE GENERATIONAL CURSES?

Just like you can inherit things genetically from your family, you can also "inherit" certain limiting beliefs, toxic behaviors, and unhealthy habits. They could be anything from warped attitudes toward food to substance abuse and dysfunctional relationships. The impact these factors have on your life may be minor or significant, but if you feel that they're holding you back in any way, you have the power to change your future and break your generational curses.

HOW TO BREAK BAD GENERATIONAL HABITS

- STEP 1: Identify. Take some time to reflect on your generational curses. Once you've identified them, you'll be able to better observe the effect they have on your life and relationships.

- STEP 2: Challenge. Set yourself some practical steps to change your behavior and safeguard yourself from the behavior of others that contributes to the generational curse. Whether that's creating new, healthy routines, prioritizing self-care, or limiting certain people's access to you, make sure your strategies are achievable and impactful.

- STEP 3: Implement. This is the hardest step. This is where you enforce the strategies you came up with in Step 2. Be prepared for resistance from other family members who may not be willing or able to accept your desire for change. Stick with it and be strong.

- STEP 4: Create. Break the mold and create new traditions, habits, and behaviors to replace the generational curse that reflects the person you are now and who you want to be in the future.

- STEP 5: Celebrate. Breaking generational curses is difficult and brave work. Remember that setbacks are normal and to be expected, and be kind to yourself on this journey. Celebrate your progress—no matter how slow—and give yourself time to heal and transform.

USE THESE JOURNALING PROMPTS TO GET YOU STARTED:

Am I the victim of a generational curse?

What can I do about it?

How does it affect me?

How to navigate conflict with your loved ones

Sometimes, spending time with your friends and family can feel less like a walk in the park and more like a sprint through a battlefield. Whether you were the one who declared war or you've been dragged into a conflict unwittingly, as you move into adulthood, it's more important than ever to learn how to respond intentionally rather than emotionally if you want to maintain healthy relationships and mental peace. Here's everything you need to know about how to navigate conflict with those closest to you.

KNOW HOW TO PICK YOUR BATTLES:
We all get irritated with our loved ones, but not every hill is worth dying on. Save your energy for the battles that truly matter to you and let the small stuff slide.

KNOW WHEN TO LISTEN:
Interrupting, talking over people, and jumping to conclusions never leads to productive solutions. Practice the art of active listening and hear people out with an open mind and a compassionate heart, even if you don't agree with them.

KNOW WHEN TO STAND YOUR GROUND:
While compromise is important, there are also times to hold firm, especially when it comes to protecting your boundaries, beliefs, and well-being.

KNOW WHEN TO BACK DOWN:
If emotions are running high and things are getting heated, consider taking a step back to cool off and regroup. Sometimes, a bit of distance and perspective can help diffuse tensions and pave the way for peace.

KNOW WHEN TO APOLOGIZE:
We all make mistakes, but being an adult means owning up to them. If you've messed up or hurt someone's feelings, swallow your pride, acknowledge what you did, and offer a genuine apology.

KNOW WHEN TO LET IT GO:
Holding onto grudges because you need to be right only serves to drag you down and poison your relationships, so sometimes it's better to be the bigger person and let it go.

KNOW WHEN TO WALK AWAY:

There may be times when conflicts with friends or family members become so toxic and all-consuming that there's simply no relationship left to repair. This is when it's time to walk away. This is an extreme final step, but you have to protect your emotional and psychological safety. This can be particularly difficult with family, as there is often an unhealthy misconception that family members are obligated to always forgive each other, no matter how badly they've behaved. Put yourself first and remember: no one gets an automatic pass into your life.

Side-stepping sibling rivalry in adulthood

When it comes to your relationship with your siblings, there are certain things you might be expecting to leave behind as you enter adulthood. Wrestling over the TV remote, fighting over who used up all the hot water, squabbling on long car journeys . . . such happy memories.

If you experienced sibling rivalry growing up, you might be expecting it to do a vanishing act now. Unfortunately, for a lot of us, sibling rivalry doesn't really disappear when we become adults, it just sort of . . . transforms. Further education, jobs, relationships, travel—there are just as many things to compete against in adulthood as there were in childhood.

Whether your rivalry comes from you and your siblings or as a result of favoritism (real or imagined) from another family member, it can be a hard mindset to escape. Follow these steps to help rid yourself of the curse of sibling rivalry.

1. DON'T ENGAGE: Whether you're the sibling who has always been favored or you feel like the one who can never measure up, just don't engage in those conversations. Shut them down as firmly as you feel comfortable doing and make it clear to your family and siblings that you want no part in it.

2. DON'T COMPARE: There is no one right path in life and there is no one right way or time to do things. Focus on yourself and your own journey and don't spend your energy worrying about what other people are doing, including your siblings. Remember that success looks different for everyone, and outward accomplishment doesn't always equal inner happiness.

3. DON'T REGRESS: We can often feel stuck in certain roles that we played (either intentionally or unintentionally) in childhood. When we spend time with our family as adults, it's easy to fall back into those old roles. This may partly be because your family is only able to see you through the eyes of the child you used to be, not the adult you're becoming, so they treat you accordingly (which can be super frustrating). It's up to you to show people how you want to be treated and not allow yourself to be sucked back into old patterns and dramas.

> "I can't change how other people behave, I can only change how I respond."

Don't forget your elders

It's easy to get caught up in your busy adult life, but it's also really important to check in on your parents and grandparents and remind them that they're still a big part of your life, too.

There's no one-size-fits-all answer for when or how often you should do this, and it will depend on a variety of factors such as what kind of relationship you have with your elders, how far away you live, and whether they have additional mental or physical health needs, but here are some vital tips to get you started:

1. QUALITY OVER QUANTITY: Even a quick phone call, a silly meme sent via text, or an I-saw-this-and-thought-of-you link to an article can bring a smile to someone's face.

2. MAKE IT PART OF YOUR ROUTINE: Whether you can fire off a few texts on your commute or you always know you've got 10 minutes for a call on your walk home from the gym, try to build regular chat time into your routine. If you're living in the same area as your parents or grandparents, why not incorporate a quick cup of joe on your way home from your weekly errands?

3. MIX UP YOUR ROUTINES: Bear in mind that your older relatives and loved ones may not be as comfortable with certain types of technology, so consider phone calls, emails, and even old-school letters (pen pals—adorable!).

4. MAKE PLANS TOGETHER: In the same way that you may need to make more of an effort to catch up with your friends now, your interactions with your relatives might not be as regular or spontaneous as they once were if you're no longer living at home. Make an effort to plan fun activities together, even if it's as simple as family dinners, nature walks, or movie nights.

5. GO ALL OUT ON SPECIAL OCCASIONS: Chances are, as a child, your parents and grandparents were the ones who made the effort to make special occasions extra magical for you. As you become an adult, it's now your chance to repay their kindness and make special occasions enjoyable for them.

Tapping into the wisdom of older generations

Every generation thinks they know best (obviously, our generation actually does know best), but remember that your parents and grandparents were once young adults, too, and some of their pearls of wisdom will be timeless. Sure, they might not know how to use FaceTime but, when it comes to the bigger questions in life and love, they might just give you the perspective you need.

On the next occasion you're spending time with your older loved ones, try throwing a few of these gems their way and see what nuggets of hard-earned wisdom come back:

1. What did you find most challenging when you were my age?
2. Who supported you most when you were growing up?
3. How did you meet friends and partners when you were my age?
4. What did love mean to you when you were my age?
5. What was your first heartbreak like?
6. How did you make decisions about school and careers?
7. How did you manage your money?
8. If you could change one big decision you made, what would it be?
9. In hindsight, what was the best decision you made for yourself?
10. What advice would you give your younger self?
11. What noteworthy world event had the biggest impact on you?
12. What do you think you and I have in common?
13. What do you think is the biggest challenge I'll face as I get older?
14. If you could grow up in my generation instead of yours, would you want to?
15. What surprised you most about adulthood?

Listen intently, actively, and with compassion. You never know, you might find out the secret to the whole thing . . .

"How to love yourself is how you teach others to love you."

RUPI KAUR

Technology

AKA THE
TECH TOWER
OF TERROR

No trip to Adult Land would be complete without an exhilarating ride through the highs and lows of technology, mostly because, well, you can't really get to Adult Land without it these days. The tickets are only available online, you can't find it without Google Maps, and you have to scan a QR code before you're even allowed in.

But you're a digital native so, of course, you made it here with no trouble at all. And now you're strapped into your seat, ready to embark on the ride of your life. As the Tech Tower of Terror ascends to soaring heights, you'll marvel wide-eyed at the incredible advancements dotting the digital landscape on the way up. You'll pass smartphones that double as personal assistants and AI tools that revolutionize the way you live, work, and play. Anything is possible and the only limit is your imagination!

BUT JUST WHEN YOU'VE REACHED THE SUMMIT, HERE COMES THE INEVITABLE PLUNGE.

They've changed the charger cable again . . . it's not called that anymore . . . your company is introducing a new collaboration platform . . . unexpected item in the bagging area . . . you have to do two-factor authentication . . . oh, and your battery's dead . . .

Keeping up with technology (on top of all the other adult-y things you've got to think about now) can feel exactly like this never-ending cycle of ups and downs—just when you've got your head around something, there's a new version, a software update, or a completely reimagined user interface that sends you hurtling toward the ground at breakneck speed, cursing the day you let the machines into your life. But love it or hate it, technology will play a part in pretty much every aspect of your adult life.

So, stick your phone on silent and devote all your attention to this next bit, as we explore all the essential aspects of technology you need to master Adult Land, from curating your online persona and protecting your privacy to getting the most out of your Sunday night scrolling sessions #lifehacks #adulting #blessed.

The ups and downs of social media

In today's world, social media platforms have become our virtual playgrounds. They put the world at our fingertips, offering a seemingly endless supply of connection, creativity, and cute cat videos at the touch of a button. But, like any playground, social media comes with its fair share of swings and roundabouts. So, let's take a scroll through the world of social media and see if we can pick up some healthy online habits to follow.

WHY WE LOVE SOCIAL MEDIA
On the sunny side of the social media street, we have the pros:

- instant connection with friends and family
- a platform for self-expression and creativity
- a wealth of information and entertainment at our fingertips.

THE DARK SIDE OF SOCIAL MEDIA
Anyone who has ever read a comments section will know that social media isn't all #sunshineandrainbows. You've also got to contend with:

- the pressure to present a curated, picture-perfect version of your life
- trolls who take advantage of the anonymity of the internet to be the worst versions of themselves and spread unsolicited opinions, nastiness, and judgment all over other people's accounts (hot take: the ones who feel the most pressure to be perfect are probably also the ones spreading the hate)
- the addictive dopamine rush you get from endless scrolling that wreaks havoc on your mental health and leads to feelings of inadequacy, loneliness, and FOMO.

MAKE SOCIAL MEDIA WORK FOR YOU
So, how can we make sure we're using social media to enrich our lives without falling prey to its pitfalls? Just remember to keep it REAL:

- **REFLECT:** Think before you post and consider the effect it has on yourself and others. Does this violate your privacy or someone else's? Does everyone need to know this about you? Would you want potential employers to see it?
- **EMPATHY:** Communicate with kindness and do your bit to make sure the accounts, brands, and ideas you promote make your little corner of the internet a better place.
- **AUTHENTICITY:** Share your true self with the world, flaws and all, and celebrate the beauty of imperfection. Remember that social media is just a highlights reel, not the whole picture.
- **LIMIT:** Set limits on your social media usage and prioritize real-life connections and experiences. Get ruthless and unfollow accounts that don't serve your mental health or bring you joy.

Taking a digital time out

Ah, the digital detox—a much-needed respite from the bright lights, distracting sounds, and anxiety-spiking notifications that haunt our waking hours. In a world where we're constantly bombarded with information and stimuli, taking a break from both social media and general internet scrolling can be a game-changer for our mental and physical health. So, let's unplug, recharge, and embrace life beyond the screen. Your mind, body, and soul will thank you for it!

WHY DO WE NEED A DIGITAL PURGE?

1. BOOST YOUR MENTAL HEALTH: This is top of the list for good reason. Without the constant barrage of social media updates and news alerts, our overstimulated minds can finally breathe a sigh of relief and enjoy a much-needed moment of calm and clarity. Taking a break from the digital noise allows us to reconnect with ourselves and our surroundings, fostering mindfulness and bringing our stress levels *right* down.

2. FOCUS ON YOUR PHYSICAL HEALTH: Instead of hunching over your screens for hours on end, unplug and get outside to move your body and soak up that vitamin D. Yes, you could lie on the couch all day sending your bestie reels, or you could invite them for a fun day hiking together along that awesome trail you've seen on Instagram.

3. SWITCH OFF TO SWITCH ON: When we're constantly glued to our screens, we miss out on the beauty and wonder of the world around us. By putting the screens away and being fully present in the moment, we can savor life's simple pleasures, connect more deeply with our loved ones, and enjoy more meaningful relationships.

THREE STEPS TO DIGITAL FREEDOM

- STEP 1: Set boundaries on your screen time. Use the Do Not Disturb options on your phone to automate your digital curfew until it becomes a habit. There are also apps you can download to track your screen time and help you stick to your usage limits.

- STEP 2: Allocate screen-free times. Go completely tech-free at certain times of the day, such as mealtimes or when you're socializing. Tell your friends and family what you're doing and encourage them to keep you accountable (plus, chances are they'll like the idea of reducing their screen time, too, and want to join in. Accountability buddies—yay!).

- STEP 3: Upgrade to a full digital-detox-weekend. Take a trip or just stay home and unwind, either way, work up to spending a full weekend without your phone (just remember to tell your loved ones what you're doing so they don't panic when they can't reach you). We absolutely guarantee you'll feel more energized, refreshed, and alive (aka not a scrolling zombie) come Monday morning.

There's an app for that

Feel like you need some extra help to adult properly? Don't worry, there's definitely an app for that. Whether you want to track your fitness goals, optimize your productivity, or pick up some new skills, why not take some time to sift through the digital haystack to find the best apps to help you seem like you know what you're doing?

HEALTH AND WELL-BEING

- Research apps that will help keep your health in tip-top condition, such as monitoring your sleeping patterns, offering guided meditations, or providing journal prompts.

FITNESS

- To keep on top of your fitness goals, search for apps which will allow you to track your calories, exercise, and progress, or even provide databases of recipes and workouts.

PRODUCTIVITY

- Discover an app which will allow you to create lists and schedule your tasks daily, weekly, or whenever you like, so you'll never miss garbage day ever again.

TRAVEL

- If you're a frequent traveler, find an app which will support your wanderlust and your budget! There are lots out there which will simultaneously find amazing deals and provide personalized alerts for the best prices for your destination.

LEARNING

- Whether you've always dreamed of speaking fluent Japanese or you just want to pick up some basic Portuguese so you can impress your cute Brazilian barista, how about finding an app which provides fun, free, and easy language learning?

SUSTAINABILITY

- There are some incredible apps out there which aim to connect neighbors and local businesses to share unwanted or spare food instead of throwing it away. Inspirational!

Handy keyboard hacks

In our busy adult lives, there's nothing we love more than a time-saving hack that saves us precious seconds we could use for something more productive (like napping). When it comes to typing, every keystroke counts, so get familiar with these useful keyboard shortcuts to streamline your tap-tap-tapping and get things done in half the time.

FUNCTION	WINDOWS	MAC
UNDO	ctrl + Z	⌘ + Z
REDO	ctrl + Y	⌘ + shift + Z
CUT	ctrl + X	⌘ + X
COPY	ctrl + C	⌘ + C
PASTE	ctrl + V	⌘ + V
SAVE	ctrl + S	⌘ + S
PRINT	ctrl + P	⌘ + P
CLOSE	alt + F4	⌘ + W
OPEN FILE	ctrl + O	⌘ + O
NEW FILE/FOLDER	ctrl + N	⌘ + N
OPEN TAB	ctrl + T	⌘ + T
REOPEN CLOSED TAB	ctrl + shift + T	⌘ + shift + T
FIND	ctrl + F	⌘ + F
QUIT	alt + F4	⌘ + Q
SELECT ALL	ctrl + A	⌘ + A
BEGINNING OF LINE	Home	⌘ + ←
END OF LINE	End	⌘ + →
BEGINNING OF DOCUMENT	ctrl + home	⌘ + ↑
END OF DOCUMENT	ctrl + end	⌘ + ↓
SEND TO RECYCLING/TRASH	Delete	⌘ + delete
FORCE QUIT/END TASK	ctrl + alt + delete	⌘ + option + esc

Staying safe online

We digital natives are hands-down the most tech-savvy generation in history, but spending so much time online can mean we get too comfortable and let our guard down. Don't forget that everything from your conversations and shopping habits to your sensitive banking information and home address is potentially up for grabs by scammers lurking in the murky corners of the internet, so you need to keep your wits about you if you want to stay safe online.

HOW TO AVOID A SCAM

First up, let's talk cyber-scams. These sneaky schemes come in all shapes and sizes, from phishing emails and fake websites to bogus calls and text messages. Follow these simple steps:

- TRUST YOUR GUT: If something seems too good to be true—like an email declaring a hefty inheritance from a long-lost family member you've never heard of—chances are, it probably is. Be wary of unsolicited emails, messages, or calls asking for personal information or money, and never click on suspicious links or download unknown attachments.

> Generally speaking, your bank will never ask for your sensitive information over the phone or via email. If you're ever unsure, call your bank yourself or visit in person to handle any issues.

- DO YOUR HOMEWORK: Before buying anything or sharing sensitive information online, take a moment to research who you're dealing with. Look for reviews, check their website for security indicators like HTTPS and padlock icons, and verify their contact information through official channels.

- KNOW THE SIGNS: Scammers are chameleons, but there are a few classic giveaways. Keep an eye out for red flags such as poor grammar and spelling and requests for urgent action or secrecy. Maybe . . . if something smells phishy . . . it probably is!

HOW TO PROTECT YOURSELF ONLINE

- STEP 1: Keep your devices and software up-to-date with the latest security patches and antivirus software (yes, we know, another expense—but it's worth it).

- STEP 2: Use strong, unique passwords for all your accounts (no, you shouldn't use the same one for everything) and consider enabling two-factor authentication for an extra layer of protection.

- STEP 3: Take the time to review and adjust your privacy settings on all your social media platforms and apps to control who can see your information and activity.

All about algorithms

Have you ever noticed how you search for something once, and then suddenly your social media streams and pop-ups are full of targeted ads for that same thing? That's just one example of how algorithms are constantly working behind the scenes to shape your online experience. Sometimes, this is super helpful, but it's not all good news . . .

WAIT, WHAT'S AN ALGORITHM?

Basically, an algorithm is a set of rules or instructions designed to solve a specific problem or perform a particular task. In the online world, algorithms are the secret sauce behind everything from social media feeds and search engine results to product recommendations and targeted advertising.

So how does this digital sorcery actually work? Well, it all starts with data—lots and lots of data. Algorithms analyze huge amounts of info about your online behavior to make educated guesses about what you might want next. They then use these insights to personalize your online experience, serving up content, ads, and recommendations tailored to your tastes and interests.

THE DANGEROUS UNDERBELLY OF ALGORITHMS

Sounds pretty handy, right? Well, hold on to your hats, because there's a flip side to getting your content spoon-fed to you. While algorithms may seem helpful, they also have the power to profoundly manipulate and impact your views, behavior, and mental health.

THE ECHO CHAMBER EFFECT: One of the biggest concerns around algorithms is that they reinforce our existing beliefs and preferences, creating a digital bubble that shields us from viewpoints and perspectives that might challenge our preconceptions.

CONFIRMATION BIAS: The echo chamber effect is just a hop, skip, and jump from a phenomenon known as confirmation bias, where we only seek out information that confirms our preconceived ideas, driving us deeper into our echo chambers and limiting our exposure to other points of view.

PERPETUATING STEREOTYPES: Algorithms can inadvertently reinforce existing biases in the content and recommendations they serve up, perpetuating harmful stereotypes—particularly when it comes to things like race, gender, and socio-economic status—and contributing to systemic inequality.

HOW TO BEAT THE ALGORITHMS

- Actively curate your feeds and seek out diverse perspectives and sources of information.

- Use your critical thinking to question the content and recommendations served up to you online.

- Change the privacy settings on your apps to stop them from tracking your behavior.

- Clear your browsing data regularly.

How to make the most of your Netflix binges

So, you've found yourself knee-deep in another Netflix marathon. No judgment, we've all been there. But this time, instead of reaching for the same old guilty-pleasure shows and movies, why not try broadening your horizons just a little and turn your next streaming binge into a chance to soak up some educational content—all from the comfort of your couch?

SCIENCE AND NATURE DOCUMENTARIES
Imagine having Sir David Attenborough take you on hundreds of mini field trips to meet every living thing on our planet—that's basically what you have at your fingertips thanks to science and nature documentaries! These captivating gems are a treasure trove of knowledge just waiting to be discovered. Whether you're fascinated by the wonders of space, the workings of the human brain, or the weirdness of life under the sea, there's something for everyone.

HISTORY DOCUMENTARIES
Even if you found history a bit of a snooze-fest in school, don't sleep on the incredible selection of history documentaries available on streaming platforms. From the rise and fall of ancient civilizations to little-known historical figures and the revolutions that shaped our world, unravel the stories of humanity's trials and triumphs and watch the past come to life in vivid detail.

MYSTERY AND TRUE CRIME
It's not just the podcast world where true crime reigns supreme. Documentaries offer a unique look into the darkest corners of the human psyche and allow you to play armchair detective, observing the complexities of criminology and the workings of the justice system. Prepare to be engrossed as you follow the twists and turns of real-life investigations, leaving no stone unturned in the pursuit of truth.

ART AND COOKING SHOWS
If true crime is all a bit grisly for you, why not step into the world of the finer things in life by indulging in a cooking or art show? Whether you want to learn about the science of food while tantalizing your tastebuds or pick up some fancy-sounding phrases to impress your date when you visit that art gallery next weekend, the world is your oyster.

TRAVEL
Speaking of which, how would you like to embark on a whirlwind adventure without having to change out of your PJs? Hands down the cheapest way to see the world, travel documentaries take you to every corner of the globe and immerse you in the sights, sounds, and flavors of fascinating cultures, uncovering hidden gems and iconic landmarks along the way.

Turning mindless scrolling into learning

Just like your streaming binges don't need to be totally mindless, you can also hack your scrolling sessions to make them a source of learning and self-improvement too (that's right, there's more to do online than watch people squeezing out their blackheads). Here's how to turn scrolling into learning and—bonus—make yourself the most interesting person in any room.

HOW TO SCROLL YOUR WAY TO SUCCESS

- READ THE NEWS: "Ugh, I already have a news app on my phone," we hear you cry. That may be true, but glancing at the news alerts or top stories that pop up on your phone isn't *really* reading the news. Take the time to read full stories and then look them up on different news sites to see how other outlets are covering them. Seeking out information from diverse sources is the best way to beat confirmation bias and keep your mind open to other perspectives.

- FOLLOW EDUCATIONAL ACCOUNTS: Build up a list of online accounts that pique your interest in areas such as science, history, and nature. There are some awesome accounts out there to keep you up to date with the latest discoveries and breakthroughs in fields like biology, physics, and astronomy, like National Geographic. Or, if you're finding modern life all a bit too much, why not lose yourself in forgotten stories from the past by researching some fascinating history accounts?

- SEEK OUT NEW VOICES: Search for accounts sharing diverse perspectives and voices that challenge your worldview and introduce you to new ideas and experiences, whether it's activists fighting for social justice, artists pushing the boundaries of creativity, or citizen journalists sharing authentic stories on the ground.

- BE A FORCE FOR GOOD: Use your scrolling time productively by engaging with online community groups to learn what's going on in your local area and find ways to share your skills, knowledge, and time to become a valued member of your community.

The fake news era

No longer an April Fool's Day punchline, these days, fake news stories run rampant, and the truth is often obscured by a thick fog of misinformation. In this fake news era, it's becoming harder and harder to sift out the truth amongst the constant barrage of increasingly convincing lies and, with the rapid rise of deep fakes, the stakes have never been higher. So how can you protect yourself from the onslaught of fake news and sort the truth from the trash?

WHAT IS FAKE NEWS?
Essentially, fake news refers to false or misleading information presented as legitimate news. It can take many forms, from outright lies and fabricated stories to misleading headlines and doctored images. The goal of fake news is generally to deceive, manipulate, or influence public opinion for political, financial, or ideological gain.

MISINFORMATION AND DISINFORMATION
As well as fake news, you may have seen the terms "misinformation" and "disinformation" floating around. They're both types of fake news, but there's a slight difference between them:

- Misinformation is false information that's spread regardless of whether there's an intention to mislead (so this could include accidentally passing on fake news).
- Disinformation is false information that's spread deliberately to be misleading, including bias, manipulated narrative or facts, and propaganda.

WHY DO WE HAVE FAKE NEWS?
There are a lot of reasons behind the rise of fake news in our world today, from highly sophisticated profit-driven and political agendas to bored trolls in their parents' basements seeing what they can get away with. Basically, anyone with an internet connection, a keyboard, and a couple of brain cells can spread misinformation far and wide, and—crucially—there are very few consequences for doing so. The simple fact is that sensationalist lies (or heavily embroidered half-truths) often seem more interesting and shareable than basic facts. As a society, our attention spans are waning and our ability to distinguish between reality and fiction is rapidly diminishing (thanks, in no small part, to our reliance on technology), creating the perfect conditions for a fake news epidemic.

Have you ever heard the adage, "A lie can get halfway around the world while the truth is still putting its shoes on"? It's an old saying, but it's just as relevant today as ever.

HOW TO STOP FAKE NEWS IN ITS TRACKS

Here's how you can sort the fact from the fiction, spot the signs of fake news and make sure you're not part of the problem by passing it on.

- STEP 1: Approach everything you read, see, or hear with a healthy dose of skepticism. Question the source, consider the author's credibility, expertise, and motives and verify the information with multiple reliable outlets before accepting it as truth and definitely before passing it on.

- STEP 2: Learn the language of fake news. Look out for sensationalist headlines, grammatical errors, and overly emotional language, as these tend to be big red flags for misinformation. Be wary of stories that try and play on your emotions (positive and negative), as these are often designed to manipulate rather than inform.

- STEP 3: Keep an eye out for comments from bots. Fake news sites often buy bots to artificially promote their content, so if you see a load of similarly worded comments on certain posts, chances are they're from a bot and the content has come from a fake news source.

- STEP 4: Call it out. If you spot a fake news story being spread around (and you can bring receipts to prove it's fake), comment on the post to let others know it's fake news and help them avoid making the mistake of believing it or passing it on. It may seem like a small victory in the raging war against fake news, but every action has a ripple effect, and the people who see your post might think twice before believing everything they read in future.

It may not seem it, but fighting back against fake news is one of the key battles of our time. Fake news plays a crucial role in how we think and act on issues such as climate change, war, and human rights. Combating fake news is not just about squashing rumors, it's about upholding the fundamental values of truth, integrity, democracy, and citizenship that are essential for our society to progress and protect our future.

Curating your virtual personality

Settle in for some social media self-reflection—it's time to take a long, hard look at your virtual personality. Everything you post, like, and share paints a picture of who you are, so it's essential to be aware of your virtual persona and how it may be perceived by your friends (or romantic interests), future employers, and the world at large.

YOUR THREE-STEP VIRTUAL PERSONALITY MAKEOVER

- STEP 1: Take a step back. In true reality-makeover-show style, we've got to start by facing some harsh truths. Try to look at your social media profiles through the eyes of an outsider—what impression do your posts, photos, and comments give off? Do they reflect your values, interests, and personality, or do they tell a different story altogether? Remember, your social media profiles will probably be the first things that come up when people search for you online, so think carefully about what you're presenting to the world.

- STEP 2: Tidy up your digital footprint. Once you've had a good look at your online persona and identified your areas for improvement, it's time to get stuck into your digital makeover. (This is the part where they go into your closet and ruthlessly gut all the items that don't highlight your assets, then give you the best haircut you've ever had in your life and throw all the food out of your fridge.) Meticulously go through your old posts, photos, and comments and remove anything that no longer aligns with your values, interests, or the person you want to be.

- STEP 3: Tighten up your privacy. The final part of your makeover is where you learn how to maintain your new and improved look so you don't fall back into your old, sloppy ways. For your digital personality, this is all about getting into the habit of being extra mindful of the information you share publicly and considering the potential consequences before you post anything that could come back to bite you in the butt. Consider creating separate accounts for professional and personal use and take the time to review your privacy settings on each platform to make sure you're comfortable with who can see, share, and comment on your posts. And with that, your digital makeover is complete. Cue emotional music . . . tears . . . roll credits.

> It can be super difficult to look at ourselves objectively. Try pairing up with a friend to do this exercise together, looking at each other's online profiles from an outsider's perspective and offering helpful feedback.

The dangers of oversharing online

Whether it's cute videos of our dogs, pics of the amazing meal we just made, or our thoughts on the latest episode of *Doctor Who*, sharing parts of our lives online has become an integral part of how we relate to one another and feel connected to the world. But there is a delicate line between sharing and oversharing, and the latter can lead to a whole heap of unintended consequences for your personal and professional life. So, let's tiptoe through the minefield of oversharing online and learn how to avoid those TMI traps.

WHAT'S WRONG WITH OVERSHARING ON THE INTERNET?

Oh, so many things. First, let's consider the permanence of the internet—something we don't always think about in the heat of the moment. A lot of people just don't realize that once something is posted online, it's out there forever, just waiting to resurface at the most inconvenient of times (yes, even if you delete it!).

You can never truly guarantee that something has been scrubbed from the internet. Once it's out there, you lose all control over how it's used and shared.

Next, you need to think about the potential consequences of oversharing online, from damaging your professional reputation and offending your friends to putting your personal safety at risk. Many people speak and behave completely differently in their virtual lives than in their real lives, but oversharing online can have serious repercussions that spill over into the real world.

When we talk about oversharing online, we don't just mean public platforms. "Private" messaging or content-sharing platforms are also vulnerable to leaks, hacks, and other people screenshotting or sharing your "private" content.

HOW TO STOP YOURSELF FROM OVERSHARING ONLINE

- Before posting anything, remember the REAL rule (page 120) and ask yourself whether this is something the whole world needs to know.

- Think of five people whose opinions you respect, and before posting anything, ask yourself, "Would I be comfortable with these people seeing this?"

- If you're ever in doubt, always err on the side of caution and don't post. It's better to be safe than sorry!

- If you know you're guilty of oversharing, nominate a trusted friend to be your Oversharing Overseer.
Tell them to call you out whenever you've overshared online (you could even put some cash in a jar each time you overshare, then at the end of the year, use it to treat yourself and your Oversharing Overseer to lunch!).

Life-changing gadgets

From smartwatches that could save your life to futuristic notepads, we are literally spoiled for choice when it comes to incredible gadgets designed to revolutionize our daily routines, improve our well-being, and thrill us in ways we never thought possible. But are they worth the hype? Get your wishlist ready as we run down our top life-changing gadgets.

YOUR DIGITAL WISHLIST

1. SMARTWATCH: It's a watch, but not as you know it. From tracking your fitness goals to staying connected on the go, these sleek, stylish smartwatches are the ultimate multitasking accessory. What's more, some types of smartwatch also boast features such as heart rhythm monitoring, blood oxygen level reading, and fall detection, and they can even enable emergency SOS contact or tracking if you get into trouble.

2. DIGITAL NOTEBOOK: Tired of lugging around heavy notebooks and endless stacks of paper? Enter the digital notebook—a lightweight, eco-friendly alternative that allows you to jot down notes, sketch ideas, and organize your thoughts with ease. Plus, with cloud syncing capabilities, you'll never have to worry about losing your work again.

3. BLUETOOTH TRACKER: Do you constantly find yourself losing your keys, your phone, your cat? Well, have we got a gadget for you. Simply attach a handy little tracker to your prized possessions and with the tap of a button on your smartphone, you'll be able to locate them in seconds.

4. WIRELESS CHARGING PAD: Say goodbye to tangled cords and messy charging stations with a wireless charging pad. Simply place your compatible device on the pad and watch as it powers up effortlessly—no cords required!

5. SMART HOME ASSISTANT: Transform your living space into a futuristic oasis with a smart home assistant like Amazon Echo or Google Home. From controlling your lights and heating to belting out your favorite tunes without you having to lift a finger, these voice-activated assistants are the ultimate sidekicks for modern-day living.

6. PORTABLE POWER BANK: Never experience the dread of a dead battery again with your portable power bank. Whether you're hiking through the Himalayas or just strolling through a supermarket, these pocket-sized chargers are a lifesaver when your devices need a boost.

7. AIR PURIFIER: With advanced filtration technology and sleek, modern designs, smart air purifiers are a must-have for anyone looking to improve their air quality and overall well-being.

8. SLEEP TRACKER: Say goodbye to restless nights and hello to restorative sleep with a sleep tracker that monitors your sleep patterns and provides insights into your sleep quality.

Decoding tech terminology

In the world of tech talk, acronyms are abound and geek speak reigns supreme. If you've ever found yourself smiling and nodding while secretly panicking when IT Support asks you to clear your cache or your date tells you they're a coding wizard, you've come to the right place.

10 TECH TERMS TO SAVE YOUR BLUSHES

1. **CODING:** Writing instructions or commands using a programming language that computers understand so you can get them to do stuff (i.e., create software, websites, and apps).

2. **THE CLOUD:** A network of remote servers hosted on the internet that stores, manages, and processes your data so you can access it from any device with an internet connection.

3. **FIREWALL:** A security system which monitors and controls incoming and outgoing traffic to protect your devices against unauthorized access and potential cyber threats.

4. **COOKIE:** A small piece of data stored on a user's computer by a website to track and remember information about the user's browsing habits and preferences.

5. **CACHE:** A temporary storage area used by web browsers to store copies of web pages, images, and other content to improve loading times and performance.

6. **VPN:** Short for "virtual private network," a VPN is a secure network connection that lets you access the internet privately and securely by encrypting your data and masking your IP address.

7. **BANDWIDTH:** The maximum amount of data that can be transmitted over a network connection in a given amount of time—basically a speed limit for your data.

8. **MALWARE:** Short for "malicious software," malware is designed to sneak-attack its way into your computers, networks, and other devices, often without you knowing.

9. **PHISHING:** A type of cyber attack where attackers try to trick you into revealing sensitive information, such as passwords or financial details, by posing as a trusted figure.

10. **ENCRYPTION:** The process of converting data into a secret code to prevent unauthorized access or interception, typically using algorithms and cryptographic keys.

DATA UNIT

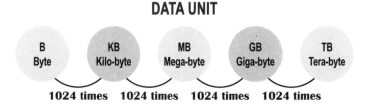

B	KB	MB	GB	TB
Byte	Kilo-byte	Mega-byte	Giga-byte	Tera-byte

1024 times   1024 times   1024 times   1024 times

"Technology is best when it brings people together."

MATT MULLENWEG

Level up your tech skills

If you haven't figured it out already (seriously, where have you been?), we are deep into the digital age, and it's pretty tough to get by these days without a comprehensive grasp of technology. More and more aspects of our everyday lives are going digital, from paying bills and booking appointments to ordering food in restaurants via QR codes. We digital natives are already pretty tech-savvy by nature, but if you want to level up your tech skills to help you stand out from the crowd as you venture out into the world of work, here are some good places to start . . .

BECOME A DIGITAL WIZARD

DIVE INTO CODING: If the idea of speaking the language of computers so you can get them to do your bidding sounds like all your Bond villain dreams come true, coding might be your calling. Whether you're interested in building websites, creating apps, or unraveling the mysteries of AI, learning to code is your ticket to harnessing the power of the machines.

MASTER THE ESSENTIALS: Think you know everything you need to about Excel, Google Docs, and Zoom? Think again. Depending on your job and lifestyle, as you move out into the world, you may find you need to master these essential everyday tools beyond the basic functionalities you've used them for in the past. Whether it's keeping track of your personal budget or delivering virtual presentations to the board of directors, these bread-and-butter tools will be like your digital Swiss Army® knife:

- Microsoft Word
- Microsoft Excel
- Microsoft PowerPoint
- Microsoft Teams
- Canva

- Zoom
- Google Docs
- Google Sheets
- Google Slides
- Adobe Acrobat Reader

- Adobe Photoshop
- Adobe Illustrator
- Dropbox
- Slack
- Asana

Check out online courses and tutorials to unlock the secrets of this essential software and help you work smarter, communicate better, and stay organized in your digital life.

Everything you need to know about AI

In recent years, the use of artificial intelligence (AI) in our everyday lives has boomed. From the moment you use facial recognition to open your phone in the morning to when you check your social media feeds before bed, AI is busy working behind the scenes to make your life a little more efficient, secure, and personalized. Let's learn a little bit about our new artificial friend so we can make sure we know how to use it responsibly.

WHAT ACTUALLY IS AI?

Artificial intelligence is when a computer does things a human would normally do, like learning, solving problems, or using language to communicate ideas. You can see examples of AI technology everywhere, and you probably use it every day without even realizing.

AI IN EVERYDAY LIFE	THIS IS AN EXAMPLE OF HOW AI CAN...
You log in to Netflix and it suggests other shows you might like.	. . . learn. AI studies your past behavior to predict your future wants or needs.
The road you usually take to get to work is closed, so Google Maps suggests another route that will get you there on time.	. . . solve problems. Navigation and mapping tools use AI to interpret real-time information about things like traffic, construction work, and road closures to work out the best way to get somewhere, so you don't have to.
You ask Alexa if you'll need a jacket tomorrow, and it replies with tomorrow's weather forecast.	. . . use language to communicate ideas. When you ask a virtual assistant a question, it uses AI to not only understand the words you say but also interpret the meaning behind them and come up with a helpful reply, just like a human would. Clever, huh?

THE PROS OF AI

SMARTER HEALTHCARE: From diagnosing diseases to personalizing treatment plans, AI is helping doctors and patients alike stay one step ahead of illness. With the power of AI, medical professionals can analyze vast amounts of data, identify patterns, and make more accurate predictions, leading to better outcomes for patients and a healthier society overall.

SAFER TRANSPORTATION: AI is driving us into the future of transportation faster than you can say "self-driving car." With AI-powered systems at the wheel, vehicles can navigate busy streets, anticipate hazards, and even communicate with each other to prevent accidents—all without breaking a sweat (or a speed limit).

PERSONALISED EXPERIENCES: From shopping recommendations to music playlists, AI is like your own personal digital genie, granting your every wish with a simple click or swipe. By analyzing your preferences, habits, and behavior, AI algorithms can tailor your online experience to suit your unique tastes, making every interaction feel like it was custom-made just for you.

THE CONS OF AI

PRIVACY CONCERNS: With great power comes great responsibility, and sometimes that responsibility includes safeguarding your data from prying eyes. As AI becomes more integrated into our daily lives, there's a growing concern about how AI systems collect, store, and use our data.

JOB DISPLACEMENT: As AI technology advances, there's a legitimate concern that some jobs may become obsolete or automated, leading to unemployment or economic instability for certain industries or communities.

BIAS AND DISCRIMINATION: AI algorithms are only as good as the data they're trained on, which means they can sometimes perpetuate or even amplify existing biases and discrimination in society. From facial recognition software to hiring algorithms, AI systems have been known to exhibit bias against certain demographics, fueling stereotypes and contributing to social injustice.

HOW TO USE AI RESPONSIBLY

- Always use critical thinking and fact-check, question, and scrutinize any information or suggestions from an AI tool.

- Read up on how the technology that powers your AI-enabled devices works so you can understand what it can do and, crucially, what it can't do.

- Keep up to date on policies and guidelines around AI use and use your voice (and your vote) to actively advocate for responsible AI practices.

Protect your tech

These days, our gadgets aren't just nice-to-have items, they're completely indispensable in our everyday lives; so there's nothing more devastating than when one of your digital extra limbs suddenly grinds to a halt. But with a little basic TLC, you can keep all your devices happy, healthy, and humming along for years to come.

HOW TO PROLONG THE LIFE OF YOUR TECH

- *ACTUALLY* **POWER THEM OFF:** Give your gadgets a break by powering them off completely when you're not using them.
- **AVOID DIRECT SUNLIGHT:** Just like vampires, gadgets don't fare well in direct sunlight (or smothered in garlic). UV rays can cause screens to fade and batteries to overheat, so keep them in the shade whenever possible.
- **KEEP IT MILD:** Extreme temperatures can wreak havoc on your gadgets, so avoid leaving them in scorching hot cars or freezing cold environments. Keep them happy by keeping them at room temperature.
- **KIT THEM OUT:** Invest in sturdy cases and screen protectors to shield your gadgets from bumps, drops, and spills. You've got your accessories, why shouldn't they have theirs?
- **DON'T IGNORE UPDATES:** Sure, software and firmware updates can be annoying, but they're there to keep your gadgets running smoothly.
- **CLEAN SWEEP:** Dust and debris can build up over time and gunk up your gadgets' gears, so give them a gentle cleaning with a soft, dry cloth to keep them in tip-top shape.
- **HANDLE WITH CARE:** Treat your gadgets like the MVPs they are—avoid rough handling and treat them respectfully to prevent damage and wear.
- **BACKUP PLAN:** Regularly backup your files to ensure they're safe and sound if the worst should happen (see the next page for tips on how to do this).

> A COMMON MYTH IS THAT YOU SHOULD LET YOUR DEVICE'S BATTERY RUN ALL THE WAY DOWN TO 0 PERCENT BEFORE YOU CHARGE IT, BUT THE OPPOSITE IS TRUE! WITH MODERN LITHIUM BATTERIES, YOU WANT TO POP IT ON CHARGE BEFORE IT COMPLETELY RUNS OUT TO PROLONG THE BATTERY'S LIFE.

WHAT TO DO WHEN YOU DROP YOUR PHONE IN THE TOILET (OR ANY WATER, FOR THAT MATTER)

- **STEP 1:** Act fast! Take it out of the water as quickly as you can (obviously) and turn it off.
- **STEP 2:** Pat it dry and shake it gently to get as much water out as possible.
- **STEP 3:** Put it inside a sealed, airtight container and cover it completely with uncooked rice or cat litter (yep, cat litter—super absorbent).
- **STEP 4:** Leave the phone for at least 48 hours. (Yes, two whole days without your phone—gasp! But this is the price you pay for playing Candy Crush on the toilet.)
- **STEP 5:** After 48 hours, remove your phone from the container, check the ports for any stray bits of rice or cat litter, then turn it on and (fingers crossed!) you'll enjoy an emotional reunion. If not, it's time to visit a professional phone doctor!

How to back up your life

If you've ever faced the soul-crushing realization that your files gone forever after your device has been lost, stolen, or damaged beyond repair, you'll be all too familiar with the importance of backing up your files. If you've avoided this horror thus far, here's how to make sure it never happens to you.

YOUR BACKUP OPTIONS

- CLOUD NINE: Take your backups to new heights by storing your files in the cloud. Services like Google Drive, Dropbox, and iCloud offer secure storage solutions that sync your files across multiple devices and keep them safe from hardware failures and digital disasters. Phew!

- PHYSICAL HARD DRIVES: If you prefer to keep your valuables where you can see them, physical hard drives will be right up your alley. Invest in an external hard drive or USB flash drive and regularly transfer your files for safekeeping. Set yourself reminders to do daily, weekly, or monthly transfers depending on your needs.

- AUTOMATE IT: Don't rely on your forgetful human brain to remember to back up your files—that's what technology is for! Take advantage of automatic backup options offered by cloud services that run in the background, ensuring your files are always up-to-date and ready for action.

- DOUBLE TROUBLE: What's better than one safety net? Two safety nets! For extra peace of mind, consider creating multiple backups using different methods. Store your files in the cloud and on a physical hard drive for double the protection against digital disasters. It's kind of like wearing a belt and suspenders—sure, it may seem a bit excessive, but guess whose pants aren't falling down?

Did you know? March 31st is World Backup Day, a day to remind everyone around the world of the importance of backing up your files (although we definitely recommend you do it more than once a year).

Community

AKA THE COMMUNITY CREW

Okay, so there's one super-important part of Adult Land we haven't covered yet. Without it, Adult Land goes from a bustling, vibrant theme park full of laughter and music to an empty, post-apocalyptic, this-would-make-a-great-location-for-a-horror-movie wasteland. No, it's not the gift shop, it's all the other people, of course! That's right, it's time to check in with the Community Crew.

In Adult Land, your community is made up of all the people who make your time here such a rich and magical experience. Imagine your colleagues as the revolving cast of staff members with their colorful costumes and unique quirks, your neighbor as the woman who runs the hotdog stand, and your barista as . . . well, the barista.

You will have already been part of one or more communities growing up—your family, school friends, neighborhood, sports teams, and so on—but, as you enter adulthood, your network is going to expand massively, especially if you're joining the workforce or heading off to college. What's more, your community is not only going to increase in size, but it's also going to increase in terms of importance to you, as you rely more and more on your community for companionship, support, and fulfillment.

But don't just take our word for it (here comes the science part): numerous studies over the years have consistently found a clear, positive correlation between the quantity and quality of a person's social ties and improved mental and physical health outcomes. So, being a member of a community not only creates an innate sense of belonging and purpose, it's also one of the most important things you can do for your mental and physical well-being.

With all that in mind, let's find out how you can be a supportive, active, and valued member of your very own Community Crew.

Oh hey, neighbor . . .

Whether you grew up with nice neighbors, terrible neighbors, or no neighbors at all, chances are you're going to have to deal with all of the above at some point as you move into adulthood. Most of the time, the type of neighbor you have will come down to the luck of the draw, but if you focus on being the best neighbor you can be, you won't go far wrong.

GOOD NEIGHBORS ARE . . .

1. FRIENDLY: Introduce yourself to your neighbors when you move in, make an effort to learn their names, and say hello or give them a friendly wave when you see them.

2. HELPFUL: Let your neighbors know you're there to lend a hand if they ever need anything, and chances are they'll return the favor to you.

3. TRUSTING: Show your neighbors you're a safe pair of hands by taking good care of anything of theirs you borrow and returning it promptly.

4. RESPECTFUL: Be mindful of your neighbors' boundaries and respect their personal space. Keep any communal areas tidy and adhere to any collective rules for the street or building.

5. CONSIDERATE OF NOISE: Sometimes, it's hard to tell how much sound travels through shared walls, so ask your neighbors to let you know if the sound from your place is disturbing them. If you're planning a party, just inform your neighbors in advance and be reasonable about how loud and late it gets.

HOW TO HANDLE A BAD NEIGHBOR

- PICK YOUR BATTLES: Figure out what you can live with and what you can't.

- CALMLY LET YOUR NEIGHBOR KNOW THE ISSUE: They may not even know there's a problem, so start from a position of assuming they're not intentionally disrupting you.

- COME ARMED WITH PRACTICAL SOLUTIONS: For example, it's not reasonable to ask your neighbor to soundproof their tuba-playing son's bedroom, but you could suggest certain hours that might be more convenient for the noise.

- ONLY COMMUNICATE IN WRITING AS A LAST RESORT: Notes of complaint can come across as passive-aggressive, but if you really can't get hold of them in person, this may be your only option. Just try to keep the tone as friendly and non-accusatory as possible.

Celebrating non-conformity and individualism

As you move into adulthood and out into the world, you're likely to come across a whole heap of interesting, unique, and amazing people who march to the beat of their own drum. You'll spot them a mile off: the entrepreneurial visionaries, humanitarian trailblazers, and outside-the-box innovators—you might even be one yourself! If you're lucky enough to have one or more of these convention-busting mavericks as part of your community, prepare to have your horizons broadened.

WHAT EXACTLY IS NON-CONFORMITY AND INDIVIDUALISM?

Non-conformity and individualism essentially means deviating from conventional norms and expectations to prioritize self-expression and your own unique values and beliefs. Non-conformists and individualists may not be interested in chasing the latest trends, following long-held traditions, or caving to societal pressures.

Non-conformity and individualism encourages independent thought, creativity, and innovation. From Leonardo da Vinci to Steve Jobs, Marie Curie to Malala Yousafzai, and Bowie to Banksy, just think of everything we wouldn't have if it weren't for non-conformist and individualist thinkers in every part of society. These people challenged the status quo and turned their unique insight into positive social and technological change. And, on a personal level, embracing non-conformity and individualism allows people to cultivate personal growth, authenticity, mental fulfillment, and live according to their own principles and passions.

HOW DO YOU EXPRESS YOUR NON-CONFORMITY AND INDIVIDUALISM?

Most of us have a dash of non-conformity and individualism in us somewhere, whether we realize it or not! You might express yours by:

* having a unique style or sense of fashion
* pursuing a non-traditional career path
* constantly thinking of ways to innovate
* having a revolutionary spirit
* questioning authority
* advocating for overlooked causes.

Gender and sexual orientations

Your identity is one of the most sacred and personal things about you. It's everything that makes you who you are and defines how you view your place in the world. A person's gender and sexual identity are a big part of their fundamental sense of self, so it's important to be informed, mindful, and respectful of how people identify.

THE DIFFERENCE BETWEEN SEX AND GENDER	
Your sex refers to the biological and physiological characteristics of people who are male, female, or intersex, such as reproductive organs, chromosomes, and hormones.	**Your gender** refers to how you identify, understand, and experience yourself and your role in society. It may or may not align with your assigned sex at birth.

PRONOUNS
Below are some common pronouns a person might use to signal their gender identity:

HE	HIM	HIS	HIMSELF
SHE	HER	HERS	HERSELF
THEY	THEM	THEIRS	THEMSELVES
ZE	ZIR	ZIRS	ZIRSELF
SIE	HIR	HIRS	HIRSELF

You may also see a combination of these, such as he/they or she/they. This means that the person is comfortable using both gendered and non-gendered pronouns.

TIP: Put your pronouns in your email signatures and social media profiles to help create a culture of inclusion and acceptance and make other people comfortable with sharing their pronouns, too.

SEXUAL ATTRACTION AND ORIENTATION
A person's sexual attraction and orientation are a result of their feelings and sense of identity, not their outward appearance—so it may not always be immediately obvious. There are many ways someone might define their sexual orientation, but here are some common ones you might come across:

- ASEXUAL: Someone who has no sexual attraction to anyone.
- BISEXUAL: Someone who is attracted to more than one gender.
- HETEROSEXUAL: Someone who is only attracted to people of another gender.
- HOMOSEXUAL: Someone who is only attracted to people of the same gender.
- PANSEXUAL: Someone who is attracted to all genders.

Be a digital changemaker

No doubt you've heard of internet trolls, tappety-tap-tapping away like angry little hamsters, filling comments sections with their unsolicited opinions and misinformation. Well, it's time to end their reign. Today's society is fast becoming the age of the digital changemakers—a revolution of people who are harnessing the power of social media and the internet to bring about positive change in the local and wider community.

WHAT DO DIGITAL CHANGEMAKERS DO?

- They promote small businesses online.

- They help find lost pets through sharing posts far and wide.

- They give away or donate unwanted items online.

- They get involved in organizing community events.

- They support charity drives.

- They promote social activism.

HOW DO I GET STARTED?

Ready to drown out the trolls and flood the internet with a wave of kindness, community spirit, and positive change? Of course you are.

- Sign up to local community groups online.

- Be active—even if that's just sharing and liking posts until you build your confidence to be more vocal.

- Keep the positive vibes!

- Leave reviews for local businesses or services you've used (this is *so* helpful!).

- Sign and share petitions to bring about positive change in your community.

- Pass along helpful information or posts.

- Volunteer your skills online. Maybe you've got a green finger or two and can help someone with mobility issues take care of their unruly garden? Perhaps you're a bit of a wordsmith and can offer to proofread job applications and other documents for recent migrants? Or maybe you're a tech whiz who can help older generations with their IT issues? Everyone has something to offer, no matter how much or how little, and volunteering has so many personal and community benefits (see page 150 to find out more).

"Be the change you wish to see in the world."

Taking it on the road

Being a good member of the Community Crew stretches far beyond your local area. We are all members of the international community, so whenever you travel, don't forget to pack your community spirit and make an extra effort to respect the cultural and social context of the place you're visiting.

HOW TO BE A RESPECTFUL TOURIST

- Read up on any cultural sensitivities and rules for the area you're visiting before you travel to ensure you don't inadvertently cause offense or get yourself into trouble. For example, as a general rule, it's always best to dress modestly when visiting religious or sacred sites.

- Support local businesses while you're there (i.e., don't just go to Starbucks) and tip if you can afford to.

- Avoid traveling in large, loud groups. Remember that you're a guest, so be considerate not to cause too much noise or disruption to other people's lives.

- Learn a bit of the language. Okay, so no one expects you to be fluent in the language of every country you visit, but learning a few phrases will go a long way to earn you some good favor as a tourist. Here are some useful words and phrases to have locked and loaded wherever you go:

Hello
Good morning/afternoon/evening
Goodbye
Yes/no
Thank you
Please
Excuse me
Sorry, I don't speak . . .

ONCE YOU'VE GOT THOSE PERFECTED, TRAVEL OVER TO PAGE 170 FOR A HANDY GUIDE ON HOW TO ASK FOR HELP IN 13 LANGUAGES.

Community spirit

You learned all about how to make new friends as an adult back on the Well-being Waltzers, and your community is a fantastic place to start. You'll already have things in common as you live in the same area, plus, it's such a great feeling to have friends living nearby that you don't have to travel halfway across the country to meet up with.

Head back to page 93 to remind yourself of those loneliness-busting tips for making new friends as an adult.

WHY YOU NEED A LOCAL CREW

- COMBAT LONELINESS AND ISOLATION: We humans are social creatures, and having a strong support network on your doorstep can go a long way to fight feelings of loneliness and isolation, especially in an increasingly disconnected digital world.

- DEEPEN YOUR SENSE OF BELONGING: Getting involved in local clubs and events can provide a real sense of belonging and connection, especially if you've recently moved to a new area, which is crucial for your mental and emotional well-being.

- EXPAND YOUR SOCIAL CIRCLE: Getting involved with activities in your local area is a great way to meet both like-minded people and people who you might not otherwise have met.

- PRACTICE YOUR SOCIAL SKILLS: Socializing in low-stakes settings with your local community provides you with opportunities to practice your social skills in a safe and supportive environment. This is especially helpful if you're shy or introverted.

- FIND MENTORS AND ROLE MODELS: Your local community will be full of people from all walks of life who could prove to be valuable mentors or role models to guide and support you in your personal and professional development.

- GIVE BACK TO YOUR COMMUNITY: Many local clubs and organizations are focused on volunteering or community service. Joining one of these clubs or teams is a great way to give back to your community and make a difference.

Putting yourself out there

So you want to start being a more active member of the Community Crew—that's great! But it can definitely feel a bit daunting at first. Whether you're looking to expand your social circle, organize community events, or launch a local business, confidence reigns supreme as your secret weapon for success.

CONFIDENCE-BOOSTING TIPS

Whether you're already naturally pretty confident or the idea of putting yourself out there in your community makes you want to retreat under your comforter, you'll soon be riding your newfound confidence all the way to the finish line by practicing these tips below.

- **FAKE IT TILL YOU MAKE IT:** Even if your stomach is a swirling tornado of butterflies, you can trick yourself (and others) into thinking you're more confident than you are by smiling, maintaining a good posture, and using open body language.

- **INTERACT WITH INTENT:** Be friendly, warm, and open when you interact with people in person and online. Kindness is contagious and people will be drawn to you (and you know what they say, you catch more flies with honey than with vinegar!).

- **SHARE YOUR SKILLS:** Offering your help or knowledge to other people is an automatic confidence lift as it boosts your self-worth and sense of purpose.

- **SET SMALL, ACHIEVABLE GOALS:** Be realistic about what you can achieve and celebrate the small wins to fuel your confidence.

- **BE CLEAR ABOUT WHAT YOU BRING TO THE TABLE:** Your skills, perspective, and voice are unique, don't ever forget that!

- **PRACTICE POSITIVE SELF-TALK:** Replace limiting beliefs with positive affirmations and focus on your qualities, experience, and strengths.

- **KEEP AN OPEN MIND:** A lot of the time, our confidence gets knocked when things don't go the way we expected. If you remove these expectations and approach your interactions with an open mind and let them unfold organically, you'll get a lot more out of them.

- **HAVE A GROWTH MINDSET:** Try to reframe setbacks as learning opportunities and watch your confidence soar each time you learn from your mistakes.

- **BE PROUD OF YOURSELF FOR TRYING:** It takes a lot of courage to put yourself out there, so whatever happens, you've already won just by giving it a go!

" **Alone
we can
do so little;
together,
we can
do so
much.** "

HELEN KELLER

Get your volunteering on

As well as donating money, giving your time to local businesses or charities is a fantastic way of contributing to your community. Whatever your particular strengths or area of expertise, everyone has something they can offer to improve the lives of the other people in their local or wider community. Get out there and give back!

WHY VOLUNTEER?

- It's a fantastic way to meet awesome, like-minded people who want to make the world a better, kinder place.
- It looks great on a résumé and can show prospective employers that you're a well-rounded, considerate, and active member of the community.
- If you're volunteering in an area that's related to your career, it's valuable work experience and a great way to network.
- You can develop or hone skills such as leadership, problem-solving, and teamwork.
- Volunteering can reduce stress, anxiety, and depression while increasing your happiness and sense of purpose.
- Volunteering doesn't only boost your mental health, but many volunteering activities keep you on your feet, improving your physical fitness too. Two for one!

PLACES YOU CAN OFTEN VOLUNTEER:

- charity shops
- animal shelters
- educational programs
- meal delivery services
- litter picking/community clean-up programs
- transport services—community services for taking people with mobility issues to appointments
- online—utilize local community groups and offer your services.

HOW TO VOLUNTEER

- Look out for posted opportunities online, in local newspapers, and shop windows.
- Many places may not have specific vacancies advertised but will be happy to add you to their list of volunteers and reach out to you when they need help.
- Be honest and realistic about your availability—don't overpromise what you can commit to.
- Be reliable—just because you're offering your time for free, doesn't mean it's okay to drop out at the last minute.

Kindness

Community conservation countdown

Outside of volunteering, there are plenty of day-to-day things you can do to improve conservation, sustainability, and environmental outcomes in your local area. Even the smallest gestures can have a huge ripple effect, so no effort is too small when it comes to protecting and preserving the local environment for yourself and future generations. Here are our top 10 ways to be a local community conservation hero.

1. CONSERVE WATER: Fix any leaks around the house, take shorter showers, install water-efficient fixtures (remember to get your landlord's permission if you're renting), and use a broom instead of a hose to clean outdoor areas.

2. REDUCE ENERGY USE: Opt for energy-efficient appliances, embrace natural lighting during the day, and turn off any lights and appliances you're not using (yes, we know your parents used to nag you about that, too, just don't tell them they were right).

3. REDUCE YOUR WASTE: Recycle everything you can—usually, your local municipality will pick up paper, plastic, glass, and metal recycling. Have a go at composting your organic waste and swap out single-use products for reusable alternatives.

4. MINIMIZE PLASTIC USE: Invest in some robust (and stylish) reusable water bottles, coffee cups, and shopping bags. Avoid products with excessive plastic packaging where you can.

5. **PLANT TREES AND NATIVE PLANTS:** Make your garden, balcony, or windowsill a mini jungle haven. If you don't have any green spaces, see if there are any tree-planting initiatives you can get involved in.

6. **SUPPORT WILDLIFE:** Put out bird feeders and bird baths, create bee-friendly habitats with native plants and say no to pesticides that harm insects and other wildlife.

7. **REDUCE CAR USE:** Depending on your circumstances, look for opportunities to swap out car travel for public transportation, biking, or walking. If you do need to drive, look into car sharing with your local crew to reduce your impact (and—bonus—start the day with some carpool karaoke).

8. **VOLUNTEER FOR ENVIRONMENTAL ORGANIZATIONS:** Now that you're all fired up by the idea of volunteering, why not channel that energy into participating in local clean-up events, maintenance projects, or wildlife conservation efforts organized by environmental organizations or community groups?

9. **SPREAD THE GOOD WORD:** Utilize your digital changemaker status to share information about environmental issues and solutions with friends, family, and community members and encourage others to join you in taking action to protect the environment.

10. **SUPPORT SUSTAINABLE PRACTICES AND BUSINESSES:** Put your money where your mouth is and support businesses that prioritize sustainable products by sourcing and promoting them online.

"You cannot get through a single day without having an impact on the world around you."

JANE GOODALL

Getting intentional about spending

Life is busy, and it seems to get even more so the older we get. This also means we can sometimes fall into wasteful spending habits and not really think about whether our hard-earned cash is going toward the things we really want to support. One way to become a powerful force for good as a member of your local and global community is to be more intentional about where you're spending your money.

SENSELESS SPENDING

- COFFEE: Do you really need that coffee every morning, or could you make coffee at home and donate that money to charity? (If you really do need to buy the coffee, consider supporting a local coffee shop with sustainably sourced beans rather than a large chain.)

- LUNCH/TAKEOUT: While it's fine (and delicious) to treat ourselves every now and then, the cost of buying lunch and dinner quickly adds up, and it's not an economical way to spend your money long-term.

- UNUSED MEMBERSHIPS/SUBSCRIPTIONS: We've all been there. The unused gym membership, the streaming service you forgot to cancel, the magazine subscription that just keeps renewing . . . Time to take back control and put that money toward something worthwhile.

- IMPULSE BUYS: This could be anything from snacks to snake plants. Whatever your kryptonite, set yourself a monthly budget to help keep these impulse purchases at bay.

- LATE FEES OR OVERDRAFT CHARGES: Ugh, admin, *we get it.* But this is just wasted money that could be so much better spent by those who need it most. Set yourself reminders on your phone to get on top of these annoying charges and reward yourself with some charitable giving.

- BRAND-NAME PRODUCTS: This is especially true when it comes to groceries, where the supermarket store-brand products are usually just as good as the more expensive stuff. On your next big grocery shop, go store-brand only and see how much you save, then donate the difference to your favorite charity. Boom.

Every day, keep in mind that every action you take has a ripple effect through your local and global community—and nowhere is this more acute than when it comes to how you spend your money. Charities can only continue to do their work with money, and a large part of that will come from donations. Money talks, so think carefully about what you want yours to say about you.

Let's hear it for democracy

The right to vote is a hard-won democratic privilege and one that's not to be taken for granted. When it comes to how and when you can vote, this will depend on your local area, but generally speaking, here are the broad strokes.

DIFFERENT TYPES OF VOTE

- AREA-SPECIFIC ELECTIONS: These include elections for local representatives.
- COUNTRY-WIDE ELECTIONS: These are elections where everyone in the country who is eligible can vote for the leader, and also on single issues in referendums.

DIFFERENT WAYS TO VOTE

Again, this will depend on the rules where you are, so do some research and make sure you're all caught up on your responsibilities. Remember, voting is a privilege, and it's an important part of being a good citizen and active member of the Community Crew.

- IN-PERSON VOTE: This is where you rock up to a voting center (often somewhere in your local area like a library or school hall) to cast your vote in person. You'll need to take a form of ID with you, so check before you go what forms of ID are accepted.
- VOTE-BY-MAIL: If you can't vote in person, you may be able to submit your vote by post. You'll need to register to vote by postal ballot and make sure you do it before the deadline.
- ABSENTEE BALLOT: If you can't vote in person or by postal ballot, you may be able to vote by absentee ballot. This is when you nominate someone to cast your vote for you in person. Again, check the rules where you are to make sure you don't miss out.

SOUNDS LIKE A LOT OF HASSLE . . . WHY SHOULD I VOTE?

When you vote, you're basically raising your hand and saying, "Hey, I care about what happens in my community and my country and my voice deserves to be heard." Voting is your chance to have a say in those big decisions that affect you, like education, healthcare, the environment, and even the rights of all the people you care about.

So don't sit on the sidelines—get out there, register to vote, and make sure your voice is heard. The future you want won't just happen; you have to make it happen.

Small talk your way to success

Ahh, the dreaded small talk. Whether you find yourself stuck in an elevator, a waiting room, or next to someone you don't know at a dinner party, the thought of having to engage in small talk can fill you with dread. But small talk is a super-important (and, let's face it, unavoidable) skill for you to master if you want to turn those awkward first encounters into blossoming friendships, potential romances, or useful contacts.

SMALL TALK SECRETS

- **DON'T AVOID SMALL TALK, EMBRACE IT!:** Think of small talk as a treasure hunt, a way to unearth interesting nuggets about another person. Like an anteater hunting for ants.

- **DON'T LINGER ON SUPERFICIAL TOPICS FOR TOO LONG:** Think of the conversation as a pyramid where you start by asking kind of boring questions and then use the other person's responses to ask more targeted and interesting questions to move up the pyramid to the juicy stuff at the top.

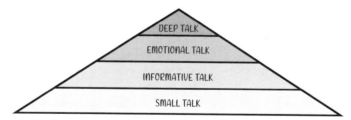

- **DON'T WASTE A FREEBIE:** In most small-talk scenarios, there will be "free" bits of information you can glean to make a connection. Stuck next to a stranger at a wedding: "How do you know the happy couple?" Standing at the bar during a Taylor Swift concert: "What's your favorite song so far?" Waiting to go into a spin class: "I've heard this instructor is tough. Have you been before?" Low. Hanging. Fruit.

- **COMPLIMENT (CAREFULLY):** People love to be complimented, but avoid coming across as creepy:

"I like your tattoos. I was thinking of getting one myself."
- makes a personal connection
- compliments their personal expression.
- opens the door for them to tell you the story behind their tattoos (if they want to).

"What beautiful eyes you have."
- creepy
- makes them edge toward the nearest exit
- something the Big Bad Wolf would say.

Be a bridge builder in your community

As you learned back on page 93 when you took a whirl on the Well-being Waltzers, adult loneliness is one of the great challenges of our time. You've looked at some tips and strategies for combating your own loneliness, but it goes without saying that becoming a force for connection within your community is a phenomenal way to combat not only your own loneliness, but that of others.

WHO IS AT RISK OF ISOLATION IN YOUR COMMUNITY?

Pretty much all of us will experience loneliness at some point, whether we've just moved to a new area, got out of a relationship, or had a close friend move away. That said, there are those within the community that are generally more susceptible to isolation, including:

- the elderly
- those with mobility challenges
- those with mental health challenges
- people who have just moved to the area
- new migrants who may be experiencing cultural and language barriers
- new parents.

HOW TO BRING PEOPLE TOGETHER

- INTRODUCE YOURSELF: Whenever you get the chance, introduce yourself to people and stop for a chat. Go and sit next to the person on the bench in the dog park and swap stories about your dogs. Tell your elderly neighbor their garden is beautiful and ask them for advice for your own garden (even if you don't need it). Ask the guy you see every day at the gym if he knows of any local running groups. Get into the habit of striking up conversations and give people your full attention. You never know what kind of a positive impact it could have on their day.

- INTRODUCE OTHERS: This is a great tip for not only improving your social and conversational skills but also helping to connect people from different parts of your life. Whenever you're at a party, work event, or just out with a friend and you bump into someone else you know, make sure you introduce them to each other and try to find a personal connection between them. You can then follow this up by connecting with them on social media or by sharing numbers (if they're comfortable with you doing that).

These are some great ways you can be a bridge builder in your community in your everyday life. When you're ready to take your loneliness-busting moves to the next level, it's time to start planning community events . . .

Planning community events

Look at you, bringing people together, tearing down those walls, and kicking loneliness to the curb. You're definitely ready to start hosting some community events, but how do you start?

SIX STEPS TO COMMUNITY EVENT SUCCESS

STEP 1: BRAINSTORM

- Think about the specific needs of your local community and start coming up with ideas of how to bring them together.
- You could post in local online community groups to get a feel for what people would like to do or browse through previous community events to see what's worked well in the past.
- Don't be afraid to start small for your first event, you can always go bigger as you gain confidence.

STEP 2: GET THE TEAM TOGETHER:

- Maybe you can plan and carry out an event all by yourself, but it will almost certainly be easier, less stressful, and more enjoyable if you bring in some supporting members of the Community Crew to help you.
- Consider partnering with local businesses and suppliers to build even more community connections.

STEP 3: MAKE THE EVENT AS INCLUSIVE AS POSSIBLE:

- Anything with a high cost associated might exclude those with financial restrictions. Don't worry about making it fancy; the point is to get people together.
- Think about accessibility for those with mobility issues.
- Consider making it child-friendly so that those with childcare considerations will still be able to attend.

STEP 4: FIND A SPACE:

- Depending on what you're doing, you might be able to use a local space like a park, recreation center, or sports hall, but check with your local council for permission first.
- Remember to consider things like parking as well as public transport accessibility for those who don't drive.

STEP 5: SPREAD THE WORD:

- Clearly advertise the details of your community event, including time, date, how to RSVP (if necessary), and any other essential information.
- Make sure you reach as many people as possible. Some community members may not be connected to the community social groups, so good old-fashioned flyers through the door are a good backup.

STEP 6: REFLECT AND ADAPT:

- After the event, gather feedback from those who attended and use this to help you inform your future events. You got this!

COMMUNITY EVENT IDEAS:

- Bring-a-dish dinners
- Dog park connections
- Local area walks/hikes
- Outdoor movie nights
- Community clean-ups
- Skill-sharing workshops
- Trivia nights
- Free fitness classes

How to be the host with the most

For a lot of us moving into adulthood, one of the things we get most excited about is finally having some independence with our living arrangements so we can have people over. Hosting can be one of the true delights of adulting, but it can also seem a little overwhelming at first. What do you cook? How do you know if you've made enough food? What if the conversation dries up? Never fear, with these tricks up your sleeve, you'll soon become the host with the most.

HOSTING 101

1. Give yourself lots of time. Like, way more time than you think you need. At least double. This includes time to plan, clean, and prepare your home as well as time to cook.

2. Make sure you know everyone's dietary requirements and allergies way ahead of time and take them into account when planning your menu, if you're serving food.

3. Keep it small—at least at first. If you're new to hosting, don't go too big too soon. Stick with a small group of friends and work your way up.

4. Keep it simple. Don't try to cook something overly impressive, and definitely don't try to cook something new for the first time.

5. Have a good selection of drink options and make sure there's plenty of water on the table. Make sure you have non-alcoholic options, too, as there may be people who don't drink or who plan to drive.

6. Spend time with your guests. They came to see you, after all. Plan your menu and your schedule so that you can mingle with your guests when they arrive instead of clattering around in the kitchen in a last-minute panic.

7. Delegate. Don't try to do it all yourself. Enlist a friend to come over a bit early to help you with the cooking, cleaning, or just to keep you sane.

8. Don't forget the playlist. You'll want some low-level background music that isn't too distracting or loud but that creates the right ambience.

9. Keep the conversation flowing. Depending on your guests, this may or not be an issue, but it's always worth having a few conversation starters, funny anecdotes, or hypothetical questions lined up in your head if you need them.

10. Have fun! Remember, the whole point of having people over is to have an enjoyable, chill time together. People would much rather have a relaxed host and a simple dinner than a seven-course, Michelin-star-level feast with a frazzled host who spends the whole night stressing in the kitchen.

Be a high street savior

There's no doubt that large chain stores pose a real threat to local businesses, but in recent years, as we've become more aware of the environmental and social impact of cheap, mass-produced imported goods, there has been a distinct trend leaning back toward supporting local businesses.

WHY SHOP LOCAL?

- **DO YOUR BIT FOR THE ENVIRONMENT:** Locally sourced products and smaller-run operations often have a lower negative environmental footprint than national or international chains.

- **DO YOUR BIT FOR THE COMMUNITY:** When you shop locally you're putting money back into your community, rather than into the pocket of a faceless billionaire. It's an investment in your community and its future.

- **GET THE BEST PRODUCE:** From fish markets and grocery stores to butchers and bakers, these businesses will often have the freshest produce (and the smallest carbon footprint).

- **GET UNIQUE PRODUCTS:** Local businesses often provide distinct products, services, and experiences that reflect the community's needs and that you can't get in chain stores.

- **GET THE PERSONAL TOUCH:** Local businesses also focus on building relationships with local people and provide an essential community link for those who are more at risk of isolation, such as the elderly.

A WEEK OF SUPPORTING LOCAL BUSINESSES

MONDAY: Switch to a local café for your morning coffee.

TUESDAY: Leave a positive online review for the awesome new coffee place you discovered yesterday.

WEDNESDAY: Buy a food basket from the family-owned deli for your mom's birthday.

THURSDAY: Visit the independent bookstore and get their recommendations for your next read.

FRIDAY: Order takeout from a local restaurant.

SATURDAY: Attend the farmer's market and pick up your veggies for the week.

SUNDAY: Reach out to a local business to organize your next community event.

Remember, even if products from local businesses are slightly more expensive than buying from large, online stores or chains, think about what your money is supporting and consider the wider impact of every purchase you make. Vote with your feet and make sure local businesses are here to stay.

Key Life Skills

AKA THE
KEY SKILLS
KIOSK

As you near the end of your whistlestop tour of Adult Land, you're probably feeling pretty confident that you've covered all the important ground: you've explored all the rides and spent some time getting to know the other guests and staff. But, before you skip merrily on by to the gift store on your way out, you may want to swing by the Key Skills Kiosk.

The Key Skills Kiosk is a magical part of Adult Land that only appears when you need it most. It's like that drawer in your house, full of random stuff like spare batteries, loose change, and chopsticks, that are somehow simultaneously absolutely vital when you need it yet instantly forgettable as soon as the drawer is shut.

The Key Skills Kiosk is positively bursting with colorful leaflets, hefty manuals, and handy how-to guides covering all the essential knowledge you need as you move through adulthood. Some of it is everyday stuff, like how to do your laundry, clean your car, and stock your cupboards. Other parts cover the stuff you need to know in the occasional tight spot, like how to get a stain out of your brother's favorite top (oops), treat a mild burn, or unclog your toilet. And some of it's the really vital stuff that will bubble up to the surface in times of emergency and make you go, "Huh? How did I know that?" (this book, that's how).

Sure, in Adult Land you'll want to experience the fun rides, not necessarily the key skills, and most of the time, you'll never even think about them. But oh boy, will you be glad they're there, lurking in the back of your mind when you need them most.

The laundry lowdown

Looking at the symbols on a clothing label or washing machine can feel like trying to decipher ancient Egyptian hieroglyphics, but once you know the symbols, it's not actually as complicated as it seems. Follow this guide to keep your clothes as squeaky clean and fresh as the day you bought them without accidentally unleashing any ancient curses.

WHAT DO THE SYMBOLS MEAN?

MACHINE WASH   30°C / 80°F   40°C / 105°F   50°C / 120°F

 30°C / 80°F   40°C / 105°F   50°C / 120°F   MACHINE WASH, PERMANENT PRESS   MACHINE WASH, GENTLE OR DELICATE

 DO NOT WASH   HAND-WASH   DO NOT WRING   DO NOT BLEACH   BLEACH IF NEEDED   NON-CHLORINE BLEACH IF NEEDED

 MAX TEMP 110°C / 230°F   MAX TEMP 150°C / 300°F   MAX TEMP 200°C / 390°F   DO NOT IRON   IRON ANY TEMP, STEAM   NO STEAM

 TUMBLE-DRY   DRY NORMAL, LOW HEAT   DRY NORMAL, MEDIUM HEAT   DRY NORMAL, HIGH HEAT   DO NOT TUMBLE-DRY

HANG TO DRY   DRIP-DRY   DRY FLAT   DRY IN SHADE

LAUNDRY RULES OF THUMB

- Always read the label first.
- Check pockets are empty before washing.
- Wash similar colors together.
- Use a mild, eco-friendly detergent.
- Use cold water for colors.
- Use warm water for white/light colors.

- Wash delicates (silk, lace, lingerie) on a gentle cycle and air dry them.
- Turn clothes inside out before washing.
- Use mesh laundry bags for small and delicate items.
- Wash your washing machine regularly (no, it's not self-cleaning).

Blockages and spillages

It might not be fun, it might not be glamorous, it's definitely not Instagrammable, but this is the stuff your adulting dreams are made of.

HOW TO UNCLOG A TOILET

- STEP 1: Stop flushing! If the water isn't draining, flushing will just keep filling the bowl until it overflows (and then you've got a whole new set of problems).

- STEP 2: Prepare. Put on rubber gloves, get your hair out of your face and lay down towels or newspapers in case things get messy. Then, roll up your sleeves and go to that happy place in your head.

- STEP 3: Use a toilet plunger to try and dislodge the clog. Place the plunger over the hole and create a tight seal. Push down then pull up firmly. Repeat a few times and then do a test flush to see if the water's draining.

- STEP 4: If plunging doesn't work (or you don't have a plunger), try these instead:

  - Pour hot water (not boiling) and dish soap into the toilet bowl (if the bowl is already full, scoop out some water first with an old jug). Let it sit for half an hour, then try flushing.
  - Pour one cup of baking soda and two cups of vinegar into the toilet bowl. Let it sit for half an hour, then try flushing.
  - Cut and straighten out a wire coat hanger to turn it into a "plumbing snake" that you can feed into the toilet bowl to try and dislodge the clog.

- STEP 5: If these steps don't work, it might be time to call in the professionals, but kudos for giving it a go yourself.

STAIN, STAIN, GO AWAY

- STEP 1: Act fast. Whatever the stain or surface, the sooner you address it, the easier it is to remove.

- STEP 2: Blot, don't rub. Blot the stain with a clean cloth or paper towel—rubbing might spread it around.

- STEP 3: Use cold water. For most stains, rinsing with cold water is a safer bet than hot water.

- STEP 4: Use gentle cleaning agents and test them on a hidden bit of the fabric first to make sure they don't damage it.

- STEP 5: Check the label on clothes or soft furnishings for specific cleaning instructions. If there aren't any, look it up online.

- STEP 6: Work from the outside in when treating a stain so that you don't spread it out further.

- STEP 7: Be patient—you might need to repeat a treatment multiple times to get the stain out.

- STEP 8: If you can't get a stain out after a couple of attempts or if you don't want to risk making it worse, take it to a professional cleaner.

Cupboard staples

Every friendship group has one friend who is always so well prepared that it's a truth universally accepted that their house is the meet-up point in the event of a natural disaster, alien attack, or zombie apocalypse. If you want to be that friend, use this checklist to make sure you're fully stocked with these essentials at all times.

- ☐ Olive oil and/or vegetable oil
- ☐ Salt and pepper
- ☐ All-purpose flour
- ☐ Sugar
- ☐ Canned goods (tomatoes, beans, fruit, vegetables)
- ☐ Dried pasta
- ☐ Rice
- ☐ Stock or broth (chicken, vegetable, or beef)
- ☐ Cereal or oats

- ☐ Tea (bags or loose leaf)
- ☐ Coffee (ground or beans)
- ☐ Long-life milk
- ☐ Lemon juice
- ☐ Honey
- ☐ Dried herbs and spices
- ☐ Cornstarch
- ☐ Baking powder
- ☐ Baking soda
- ☐ White vinegar
- ☐ Aluminium foil

- ☐ Plastic wrap
- ☐ Cleaning cloths or sponges
- ☐ Dish soap
- ☐ Trash bags
- ☐ Kitchen towels
- ☐ Rubber gloves
- ☐ Matches or a lighter
- ☐ Batteries
- ☐ Candles or a torch

CUPBOARD STAPLES

Have you got any cupboard essentials of your own to add to the list?

- ☐ ....
- ☐ ....
- ☐ ....
- ☐ ....
- ☐ ....
- ☐ ....

- ☐ ....
- ☐ ....
- ☐ ....
- ☐ ....
- ☐ ....
- ☐ ....

- ☐ ....
- ☐ ....
- ☐ ....
- ☐ ....
- ☐ ....
- ☐ ....

Finessing your food storage

If you've ever felt the pain of spending your hard-earned cash on filling up your fridge with healthy (or not-so-healthy) treats, only to find that things have gone moldy, smelly, or soggy before you've had a chance to enjoy them, this one's for you. Here's a quick run-through of how you should be stocking your fridge for maximum hygiene, freshness, and longevity.

REFRIGERATION RULES

- **THE TOP OF THE FRIDGE . . .**
  . . . has an average temperature of 7°C (45°F), making it the best place to store things like butter, hard cheese, fresh cakes, and desserts.

- **THE MIDDLE OF THE FRIDGE . . .**
  . . . usually stays at the optimum temperature of 4–5°C (40°F). This is where you want to store your fresh fish, cooked meat, eggs, and dairy products like soft cheese, cream, and yogurt.

- **THE FRIDGE DOOR . . .**
  . . . is great extra storage for all your sauces, milk, and juices. Just remember to keep the perishable stuff near the middle-to-bottom (the coldest part) and the heaviest items (like water bottles and wine bottles) at the very bottom so they don't topple out when you open the door.

- **THE BOTTOM OF THE FRIDGE . . .**
  . . . is the coldest part of the fridge, usually maintaining a temperature of around 3°C (37°F), so this is the best spot for raw meat and chilled ready meals.

- **THE DRAWERS . . .**
  . . . generally have a higher temperature of 8–10°C (48°F), so this is where you want to pop your fresh fruits, vegetables, and salad.

TASTY TOP TIPS FOR FOOD STORAGE

1. Don't keep bread in the fridge or it will go stale too quickly. If you can't get through a whole loaf before it goes mouldy, store slices in the freezer—you can pop them straight into the toaster frozen.

2. Store fresh fruit, veggies, and salad in airtight containers or glass jars lined with paper towels to help absorb moisture and stop them going soggy (ew).

3. Treat your herbs (and certain veggies) like a bunch of flowers. Pop fresh herbs, spring onions, asparagus, leeks etc. into a glass with a little bit of water. Change the water daily to keep them fresh.

4. Keeping apples and bananas near your unripe avocados will help them ripen more quickly. Avo toast for everyone!

5. Nuts and seeds actually have a best-before date and won't survive indefinitely in your cupboard (who knew?). Keep them fresher for longer by storing them in the fridge.

Around the world (solo) in 18 tips

Travel is one of the true joys of adult life, but traveling on your own (especially for the first time) can be pretty daunting. Never fear, intrepid explorers, with a bit of preparation, good old-fashioned common sense, and these handy tips, you'll be globetrotting with the confidence of a seasoned traveler before you can say, "One ticket to paradise, please."

1. Research your destination and learn about the local customs, culture, and any potential safety issues before you go.

2. Try to plan your flights or travel so that you arrive at your destination during the daytime.

3. Share your itinerary with your friends or family so they know where you're going and when you expect to return.

4. Keep your phone (and power bank) charged and accessible so you can stay in touch with loved ones or call for help if needed.

5. Dress simply and avoid outward displays of wealth; for example, a designer bag or expensive watch, as this might make you more of a target for pickpockets.

6. Choose reputable accommodation, as well as tour and transport services with good reviews (look out for user reviews that specifically mention safety).

7. Check your phone service's overseas data options and make sure you know how to turn on overseas roaming in an emergency.

8. Get an old-school paper map of the area in case your phone battery runs out.

9. If you're ever in a situation that feels in any way unsafe or uncomfortable, listen to your gut and immediately remove yourself from it.

10. Know your strengths and limits; for example, if you know you have a terrible sense of direction, don't embark on a solo three-day hike up a remote mountain.

11. Be hyper-aware of your surroundings, especially in crowded or unfamiliar areas, and avoid risky situations or suspicious individuals.

12. Carry only essential items with you and keep your valuables like your passport, cash, and devices secure in a money belt or hidden pouch.

13. Scan or photocopy your important documents (such as your passport and visa) in case your documents get lost or stolen during your trip.

14. Stick to well-lit and populated areas and avoid walking alone at night. Consider using public transport or arranging for a safe ride back to your accommodation.

15. Learn basic phrases in the local language—revisit page 146 and check the next page for some handy phrases to know before you go.

16. Avoid excessive alcohol consumption, especially when traveling alone, as it can impair your judgment and make you more vulnerable to risks.

17. Keep your eye on the local news, weather conditions, and any travel advisories or warnings for your destination.

18. Always carry emergency contact information, including your emergency contacts, local authorities, and your embassy or consulate, in case you need assistance.

How to ask for help in 13 languages

Whether you're traveling with friends, family, a partner, or going solo, you never know when you might find yourself in a sticky situation where you need to ask a local person for help—and you shouldn't always assume they'll speak your language. Here's how to ask for help in 13 foreign languages, plus some extra space for you to write the phrase in any other languages you need for your travels.

LANGUAGE	CAN YOU HELP ME?	PHONETIC BREAKDOWN
French	Pouvez-vous m'aider?	Poo-veh vooz meh-day
German	Kannst du mir helfen?	Kuh-nst doo meer hell-fen
Dutch	Kun je me helpen?	Koon yuh meh help-un
Spanish	¿Me puedes ayudar?	Meh pway-des ah-yoo-dar
Italian	Mi potete aiutare?	Mee poh-teh-teh ah-yoo-tah-reh
Portuguese	Pode me ajudar?	Poh-duh meh ah-joo-dahr
Russian	Вы можете помочь мне?	Vy mo-zhe-te po-moch' mne
Arabic	هل بإمكانك مساعدتي؟	Hal bi-iim-ka-nik musa-a-da-ti
Swahili	Unaweza kunisaidia?	Oo-nah-weh-zah koo-nee-sah-ee-dee-ah
Indonesian	Bisakah kamu membantuku?	Bee-sah-kah kah-moo mem-ban-too-koo
Japanese	手伝って頂けますか？	Te-dan-te itadakemasu ka
Korean	도와주세요?	Do-wa-ju-se-yo
Mandarin	请问, 你可以帮我吗	Qǐng-wèn, nǐ kě-yǐ bāng wǒ ma

What to do if your passport is lost or stolen

If you traveled overseas as a kid, the grown-ups on the trip probably obsessed over your passport more than Gollum obsessed over the ring, but as an adult, you are now solely responsible for the one travel document to rule them all. If your passport gets lost or stolen, it can be very tempting to go into full panic meltdown mode, but if you stay calm and act fast, you can limit the damage.

BEFORE YOU TRAVEL

- Make a high-quality digital scan and a physical photocopy of your passport and keep it in a different place to where you keep your passport (i.e., don't keep them both in a travel wallet in case it gets stolen). If your passport has been stolen, you may be able to use a photocopy in its place in emergencies.

- Consider getting travel insurance that covers lost or stolen passports.

AS SOON AS YOU NOTICE YOUR PASSPORT IS MISSING

- DON'T PANIC: Losing your passport can be scary and stressful, but staying calm will help you think clearly and act quickly.

- CONTACT THE POLICE: Whether your passport is lost or stolen, report it to the local police as soon as possible. They can provide you with a police report, which you might need in order to get a new passport.

- CONTACT YOUR EMBASSY OR CONSULATE: They can provide you with guidance on what to do next and help you get a replacement passport.

- FILL OUT A LOST PASSPORT FORM: Your embassy or consulate might ask you to fill out a lost passport form (aren't you so glad you have all your passport details to hand in a digital scan or photocopy?).

- GET A TEMPORARY TRAVEL DOCUMENT: Your embassy or consulate may issue you a temporary travel document that will allow you to return home or continue your travels.

- FOLLOW INSTRUCTIONS: Listen carefully and make notes of any guidance or requirements from your embassy or consulate, including attending appointments, paying fees, and providing necessary documentation.

- STAY IN TOUCH: Keep in regular communication with your embassy or consulate throughout the process of obtaining a new passport. They can update and assist you as needed.

> If your passport was stolen along with your wallet or bag, remember to take the necessary measures to secure or replace any other sensitive items or materials, such as freezing or canceling credit cards, changing passwords, and getting replacement keys or access cards for accommodation.

The car maintenance mini-manual

For a lot of people, getting a car is like getting a ticket to freedom and independence, but that ticket also comes with major responsibility. Keeping up with your car maintenance is vital for your safety (and the safety of your passengers and other road users), may just save you some cash in the long-run, and will definitely contribute to that warm, fuzzy, adult-y feeling of being on top of things.

EXTERIOR: Regularly wash your car and clean the interior to prevent dirt and debris from causing damage or corrosion; wax it every two to three months to keep it shiny.

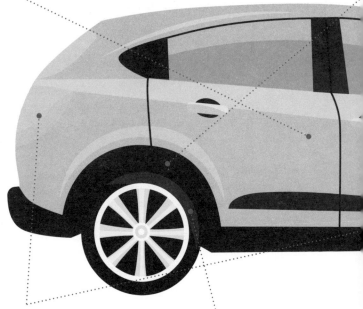

LIGHTS AND SIGNALS: Regularly check your vehicle's headlights, taillights, turn signals, brake lights and hazard lights to ensure they are working properly. Replace any burned-out bulbs promptly.

TIRE PRESSURE: Check your tire pressure once a month or before long trips with a tire pressure gauge and ensure it matches the recommended pressure listed in your vehicle's owner's manual or on the driver's side door jamb.

AIR FILTERS: Check your vehicle's air filter regularly and replace it if it's dirty or clogged. A dirty air filter can reduce engine performance and fuel efficiency.

BRAKES: Check your vehicle's brake pads and rotors for signs of wear. Replace brake pads if they're worn down or if you notice any squealing or grinding noises when braking.

BATTERY: Inspect your vehicle's battery terminals for corrosion and ensure they're clean and tight. Test your battery's voltage periodically and replace it if it's weak or nearing the end of its lifespan.

FLUID LEVELS: Regularly check your vehicle's fluid levels, including engine oil, transmission fluid, brake fluid, power steering fluid, and coolant. Top up as needed and look for any signs of leaks.

BELTS AND HOSES: Check your vehicle's belts and hoses for signs of wear, cracks, or leaks and replace any that show signs of damage.

OIL: Check your vehicle's owner's manual for the recommended oil change interval. Typically, it's recommended to change the oil every 5,000–7,500 miles, or every six months, whichever comes first.

TIRE WEAR AND TEAR: Check your tires for signs of uneven wear, cracks or bulges. Rotate your tires according to your vehicle manufacturer's recommendation, typically every 80,000–120,000 km (5,000–7,500 miles).

What's in your trunk?

If the trunk of your car would make a hoarder blush, it's time to give it a proper clear-out and replace the empty takeout containers with all these adult essentials.

YOUR CAR TRUNK CHECKLIST:

- spare tire in good condition, along with a tire jack and lug wrench for changing a flat tire
- tire pressure gauge to check your tire pressure regularly and ensure safe driving
- jumper cables in case you need to jump-start your car if the battery dies (make sure you know how to use them safely)
- first-aid kit with bandages, antiseptic wipes, adhesive tape, gauze pads, scissors, and tweezers.
- flashlight or headlamp with spare batteries
- reflective triangles to make your vehicle more visible to other drivers in case of an emergency on the roadside at night
- blankets
- bottled water and non-perishable snacks
- multi-tool or toolbox
- portable air compressor to help inflate a flat tire or top up tire pressure
- windshield washer fluid
- de-icer and ice scraper
- rain poncho or waterproof jacket (preferably with a refective element)
- paper towels, wet wipes, and hand sanitizer
- paper maps or a separate GPS device in case your phone loses signal or the battery dies
- carrier bags and reusable shopping bags.

WHAT TO KEEP IN YOUR GLOVE COMPARTMENT:

- emergency contact information, including roadside assistance, insurance company, and family or friends
- car documents, including insurance information and any necessary permits or licenses
- emergency cash in case you need to pay for fuel, tolls, or other unexpected expenses in areas where card payments may not be accepted.

"It's better to have it and not need it, than to need it and not have it."

Basic first aid

Whether it's a cooking mishap, a sports injury, or just Clumsy Colin at work burning himself on the teapot again, knowing how to administer proper first aid is the first line of defense against pain, discomfort, and infection. Here's a crash course in basic first aid techniques, but remember, if in any doubt, always call the emergency services for additional support and guidance.

HOW TO CLEAN AND DRESS A WOUND

1. Wash your hands with soap and water or hand sanitizer.
2. Gently clean the wound with mild soap and water, removing any dirt or debris.
3. Pat the area dry with a clean cloth or sterile gauze.
4. Apply an antibiotic spray or cream to help prevent infection.
5. Cover the wound with a sterile adhesive bandage or dressing.

HOW TO PUT SOMEONE IN THE RECOVERY POSITION

1. Lay the person on their back, making sure they're flat on the ground.
2. Kneel beside the person and place the arm closest to you at a right angle to their body, with the elbow bent and the palm facing up.
3. Take their other arm and place it across their chest, with the back of the hand against their cheek closest to you.
4. Bend the person's nearest leg at the knee, keeping their foot flat on the ground.
5. Using your other hand, gently roll the person onto their side by pulling their bent knee toward you, ensuring their head is supported by their extended arm.
6. Adjust their top leg to ensure their hips and knees are bent at right angles.
7. Tilt their head back slightly to keep the airway open and check for breathing and responsiveness.

HOW TO STOP BLEEDING

1. Apply direct pressure to the wound with a clean cloth or sterile gauze pad.
2. Elevate the injured area above the level of the heart if possible to reduce blood flow to the wound.
3. Maintain pressure on the wound until the bleeding stops or medical help arrives.

HOW TO TREAT MINOR BURNS

1. Remove any clothing or jewelry near the burn, but don't remove anything that's stuck to the burned skin.
2. Run cool water over the affected area for at least 10–20 minutes to stop the burning.
3. Cover the burn with a sterile gauze bandage or clean cloth to protect it from infection.
4. Seek immediate medical attention for severe burns, burns covering a large area of the body, or burns to the face, hands, feet, or genitals.

How to perform CPR

Did you know that sudden cardiac arrest is one of the leading causes of death in the world? Scary, right? If you ever find yourself faced with someone going into cardiac arrest in front of you, performing CPR (cardiopulmonary resuscitation) can buy crucial time until medical help arrives. So, pay close attention, what you're about to learn might just save a life one day.

STEP-BY-STEP HANDS-ONLY CPR

1. Check for responsiveness by gently shaking the person and calling their name (if you know it) or shouting, "Are you okay?"

2. If the person is unresponsive and not breathing normally, call emergency services immediately (or get someone else to call emergency services while you begin CPR).

3. Position the person so they are lying on their back with their arms down by their sides, with their head tilted slightly back to ensure their airway is open.

4. Begin chest compressions by placing the heel of one hand on the center of the person's chest and interlocking your other hand on top.

5. Push down hard and fast, aiming for a rate of about 100–120 compressions per minute.

6. Continue cycles of chest compressions and rescue breaths until help arrives or the person starts breathing normally.

Without a hint of irony in sight, the Bee Gees' song *Stayin' Alive* is the perfect song for maintaining the 100–120 compressions per minute sweet spot when performing CPR. But if disco's not your groove, here's a list of other songs you can sing in your head to help you keep that life-saving rhythm (you can even find dedicated CPR playlists online—what a time to be stayin' alive).

- *Eye of the Tiger* by Survivor
- *Dancing Queen* by ABBA
- *Sweet Home Alabama* by Lynyrd Skynyrd
- *Crazy in Love* by Beyoncé (feat. Jay-Z)
- *Flowers* by Miley Cyrus
- *Dance the Night* by Dua Lipa
- *The Man* by Taylor Swift
- *Dance Monkey* by Tones and I
- *Something Just Like This* by The Chainsmokers and Coldplay

How often should you change your bedsheets?

There are very few pleasures in life that beat sleeping in fresh sheets (*chef's kiss*), and in an ideal world, we'd probably all have freshly washed bedding every night. But alas, we live in the real world (one where you're also doing all your own laundry now), so what's a realistic goal to aim for fresh-sheet frequency?

> Note that this is just a guide, and you may want to clean your bedding more frequently depending on things like the climate where you are and your personal preferences.

- **PILLOWCASES—ONCE A WEEK**
  Ideally, you want to be changing your pillowcases every week. This will help to keep your pillows free of any build-up of sweat, oils, and dirt which can lead to skin problems.

- **SHEETS AND COMFORTER COVERS—TWICE A MONTH**
  If you have allergies or skin sensitivities, sweat heavily, or have been ill, you may want to change your sheets and comforter covers more frequently to prevent bacteria and odors from building up.

- **MATTRESS PROTECTOR—EVERY ONE OR TWO MONTHS**
  A mattress protector will extend the lifespan of your mattress (and they are expensive things to replace!) and protect it from spills, stains, and allergens.

- **BLANKETS AND COMFORTER—ONCE EVERY TWO MONTHS**
  Wash your comforter and any throw blankets every month or so, or more frequently if they get stained or if you have pets that sleep on the bed.

- **PILLOWS—EVERY THREE TO SIX MONTHS**
  Wash pillows every three to six months, or more frequently if they become stained or develop odors. Follow the manufacturer's instructions for washing pillows, as some may be machine washable, while others may require dry cleaning or spot cleaning.

- **MATTRESS—EVERY THREE TO SIX MONTHS**
  Vacuum your mattress regularly to remove dust, debris, and allergens. Rotate or flip your mattress every quarter to half a year to prevent sagging and prolong its life-span.

How to boil an egg

Whether you're a whizz in the kitchen or a hopeless disaster, you can't really call yourself a true adult until you've mastered the mighty boiled egg. Now, it might take a little trial and error to figure out your optimum consistency and nail your technique, but once you do, the feeling of accomplishment is egg-squisite.

FIVE STEPS TO BOILED EGG PERFECTION

1. Put the saucepan on a high heat and bring the water to a boil.

2. Lower the egg gently into the boiling water (you can use a spoon for this).

3. Start your timer (see table below) and let your eggs cook for 2–10 minutes, depending on how runny or set you want them to be.

4. As soon as the time is up, drain the water and put the eggs into some ice-cold water. The longer they sit in the cold water, the easier they'll be to peel.

BOILING TIME	YOLKS	WHITES
2-4 MINUTES	Soft, runny	Soft, runny
5-7 MINUTES	Soft but set	Firm
8-10 MINUTES	Fully set	Fully set

Before you boil your egg, check if it's out of date by doing this simple fresh egg test. Gently pop your uncooked eggs into a jug of cool water, and whether they float or sink will tell you how fresh they are:

FRESH   1 WEEK OLD   2-3 WEEKS OLD   VERY OLD

Managing your precious time

Adulthood is a busy business, and there may be times when you just feel that there aren't enough hours in the day to stay on top of all the things you suddenly need to do. Now is the time to really hone your time management skills, so check out these simple strategies to improve your productivity, reduce stress, and crush your goals.

TEN TIME MANAGEMENT TIPS

1. PRIORITIZE, PRIORITIZE, PRIORITIZE: Work out the most important tasks that need to be done and focus on getting them out of the way first before moving on to less urgent ones.

2. MAKE LISTS: Create to-do lists to organize your tasks and keep track of what needs to be done. Break down larger tasks into smaller, more manageable steps to make them less overwhelming.

3. SET SMART GOALS: Set yourself specific, measurable, achievable, relevant, and time-bound goals. Whether they're daily, weekly, or monthly goals, make sure they're realistic and take you closer to your overall objectives.

4. USE A PLANNER OR CALENDAR: Don't try and keep it all in your head, use a print or digital scheduling tool or app to plan and schedule your tasks and appointments.

5. TRY THE POMODORO METHOD: This is a time management technique where you break work into 25-minute intervals, followed by a 5-minute break. Once you've completed four consecutive work intervals, you can reward yourself with a longer break (yay!).

6. ESTABLISH ROUTINES: Developing daily routines and habits can streamline your days, save you time and energy, and reduce your mental load by limiting how many decisions you need to make in a day.

7. AVOID MULTITASKING: Many people wrongly think multitasking makes them efficient, but it can actually decrease your productivity. Focus on doing one task at a time and give it your full attention before moving on to the next.

8. SET BOUNDARIES: Learn to say no to tasks or commitments that don't align with your goals or priorities. Setting boundaries can help you protect your time and allow you to focus on what's truly important.

9. TAKE BREAKS: You're not a robot; you need regular breaks throughout your day to rest and recharge mentally and physically. Try short walks, stretching, and meditation to improve your focus, productivity, and overall well-being.

10. BE KIND TO YOURSELF: At the end of every day, remind yourself that you did your best that day and that your life isn't measured by what you achieve, but by your peace and happiness.

How to smash your gardening goals

Whether your gardening ambitions include nurturing your balcony jungle, growing your own veggies in a garden, or just doing your bit to keep a shared green space tidy and weed-free, here are the essential tools and tips you need to smash your gardening goals.

YOUR GARDEN TOOLKIT

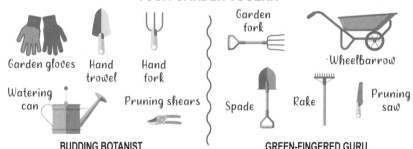

Garden gloves   Hand trowel   Hand fork   Garden fork   Wheelbarrow

Watering can   Pruning shears   Spade   Rake   Pruning saw

BUDDING BOTANIST   **GREEN-FINGERED GURU**

HOW TO NIP WEEDS IN THE BUD

1. First, make sure it definitely is a weed. If you spot something growing where it shouldn't be, there's a very good chance it's a weed, but look it up online (yes, there's an app for that) before you go into full exterminator mode.

2. Use your hand trowel to carefully dig out the weeds by hand, making sure you get all the roots.

3. To stop weeds growing among your plants, consider investing in weed fabric or mulch to lay around your plants, which will prevent weed growth and keep moisture in the soil. Planting close together will also give weeds less opportunity to take root.

4. To stop weeds growing between bricks and paving stones (i.e., where you don't want any greenery at all), use this eco-friendly weed killer recipe:

Ingredients:
- 16 cups of white vinegar
- 1 cup of salt
- 1 tablespoon of liquid dish soap

Method:
- Add ingredients into a spray bottle and shake to combine.
- Wait for a sunny spell (the rain will wash the solution off and undo all your hard work).
- Spray the solution directly onto the weeds (making sure not to spray any plants you don't want to kill!).
- Repeat as necessary.

How to be a good witness

Witnessing a crime can be an unnerving and overwhelming experience at any age, but as an adult, it's even more important to know how to act to take care of yourself and others and to know what details to look out for so that you can help the victims and authorities after the fact.

DURING THE CRIME

- **SAFETY FIRST:** The most important thing in any situation is to ensure your own safety and the safety of others. If it's safe to do so, move to a secure location away from any danger.

- **CALL FOR HELP:** If you can do so without endangering yourself, call emergency services to report the ongoing incident and provide them with as much information as you can. Depending on where you are in the world, you may also be able to send a text message to the emergency services if it's not safe to talk—check the options where you are (like, right now, go do it).

- **STAY QUIET:** If you're unable to move away from danger, stay as calm and quiet as possible and immediately turn your phone on silent.

- **BE OBSERVANT:** Make a mental and then physical note of the following list of things in as much detail as you can. (Be extremely wary of taking photos or video footage of an ongoing incident—if the perpetrator spots you filming, it could endanger you.)

AS SOON AS IT'S SAFE TO DO SO, MAKE A DETAILED NOTE OF . . .

- **LOCATION:** Include street names and any landmarks, such as nearby businesses. Note the direction that people or vehicles entered and exited the scene.

- **TIME AND DATE:** Be as precise as you can, as this information can be crucial for authorities to investigate and corroborate details.

- **DETAILED DESCRIPTIONS OF THOSE INVOLVED:** This could include clothing, height, build, accent, hair color, and any distinctive features, such as tattoos or scars, as well as anything you heard them say or noticed about their behavior before, during, or after the event.

- **VEHICLE DESCRIPTIONS:** If a vehicle was involved, note as much detail as you can about the license plate number, make, model, and color, as well as any distinguishing features, such as bumper stickers or damage.

- **WEATHER CONDITIONS:** This kind of information can be particularly relevant for road traffic accidents.

- **WITNESSES:** Look around to see if there are any other witnesses to the incident. If possible, exchange contact information with them in case the authorities need to follow up with them later.

- **LITERALLY ANY OTHER DETAILS:** Sometimes, we don't know what we've seen or heard that might be significant when it comes to investigating a crime. Write down absolutely everything and anything you remember from before, during, or after the event, no matter how irrelevant it seems.

Basic self-defense

Of course, we all hope we'll never be in a situation where we need to physically defend ourselves, but learning some simple self-defense tips and techniques can help us feel empowered and prepared in case we ever need them.

AVOID PHYSICAL CONFRONTATION IF YOU CAN

Most attackers will purposefully target someone they think they can physically overpower, so if you find yourself in a dangerous situation, your first line of defense is to try and avoid a fight altogether.

- Run away if you can.
- Make as much noise as possible and call for help.
- Stand with your feet planted firmly hip-width apart, your core braced, and your arms held out in front of you to create space between you and your attacker. This is called the "ready stance" and may just be enough to show your attacker that you're not an easy target and cause them to back off.

FIGHT, IF IT'S YOUR ONLY OPTION

If you have no option other than to fight your attacker, fight with everything you have. The most vulnerable areas for your attacker are the groin (no surprises there) and the eyes, nose, mouth, and throat. Striking these areas gives you the best chance of slowing down, stunning, or disabling your attacker long enough for you to run away and get help.

1. **FRONT KICK TO THE GROIN**: Stabilize yourself in the ready stance. Swing your dominant leg forward with as much force as you can to kick your attacker in the groin with your foot or shin. If your attacker is very close to you, drive your knee into their groin instead.

2. **PALM-HEEL STRIKE**: Start in the ready stance. Flex the wrist of your dominant hand, keeping your palm flat and your fingers pointed straight up. Thrust your dominant arm straight out as firmly as you can to jab upward at the attacker's nose or under their chin. Then, immediately recoil your arm, returning to the ready stance.

3. **HEEL STOMP**: If your attacker comes at you from behind, plant your feet firmly on the ground to stabilize yourself as best you can. Bend your knees slightly, then lift your dominant leg, point your toes up slightly, and bring your heel down to stomp onto the attacker's foot with as much force as you can.

4. **ELBOW STRIKE**: Stabilize yourself as best you can by planting your feet firmly on the ground and bracing your core. Bend your arm at the elbow, shift your weight forward, and strike your elbow into your attacker's neck, jawline, chin, or temple.

5. **KEY JAB**: Grasp your keys in a tight fist in your dominant hand with the sharpest parts of the keys sticking out from the outer edge of your fist (poking out from under your pinky finger). Plant your feet firmly on the ground and thrust your hand downward toward your attacker as sharply as you can.

Cheat Sheets

AKA THE
CHEAT SHEET
GOODY BAG

As we come to the end of our tour of Adult Land, we have a few little souvenirs for you to take away and store somewhere safe (yay, freebies!). Inside your Adult Land Cheat Sheet Goody Bag are some final pearls of adult wisdom that probably never even crossed your mind but that will definitely come in handy at some point.

Stick them on the fridge, file them neatly in a drawer, or sleep with them under your pillow, whatever you do, don't lose these helpful little nuggets—you never know when they'll be exactly what you need to get you out of a pickle . . .

What to write in greetings cards

Have you noticed as you get older that suddenly there seems to be a new greetings-card-worthy occasion every week? Birthdays, promotions, engagements . . . you can barely keep up! And just when you've found the perfect card, you then need to figure out the perfect message, one that feels personal, strikes just the right tone for the occasion, and lands all the right jokes—all while trying not to mess up your handwriting. Luckily for you, we've compiled some phrases and prompts to get your creative juices flowing so you can write cards that everyone will look forward to reading.

BIRTHDAY CARDS
- "Many happy returns . . ."
- "I'm so grateful to have you in my life . . ."
- "I'll never forget the time . . ."
- "Here's to another year filled with . . ."
- "I hope you have a fantastic time on your special day . . ."

ENGAGEMENT/WEDDING CARDS
- "Congratulations on your engagement/wedding!"
- "I'm so happy for you both . . ."
- "May your love grow stronger with each passing day . . ."
- "Enjoy this exciting new chapter in your life together . . ."
- "Wishing you a lifetime of love, laughter, and happiness . . ."

GET WELL SOON CARDS
- "So sorry to hear you're unwell . . ."
- "Sending healing thoughts your way . . ."
- "Let me know if there's anything I can do . . ."
- "Wishing you a speedy recovery . . ."
- "Take care of yourself and know that you're in my thoughts . . ."

SYMPATHY/LOSS CARDS
- "I'm so sorry for your loss . . ."
- "I can't imagine how difficult this must be for you . . ."
- "I'll always remember . . ."
- "Please know that I'm here for you, anything you need, day or night . . ."
- "Sending you strength, courage, and love as you come to terms with your loss . . ."

How to help someone dealing with loss

Dealing with a bereavement is perhaps one of the most difficult challenges life can throw our way, and watching someone you care about suffer through a loss can be very painful. Of course, there is no one correct way to support someone through grief, but the following tips are a good starting point for you to be a source of solace and strength to your loved ones in their darkest hours.

WHEN SOMEONE IS DEALING WITH LOSS ...

* BE PRESENT: Simply be there for them and give them comfort and support. Spend time with them and offer a listening ear without judgment.

* VALIDATE THEIR FEELINGS: Let them know that it's okay to feel whatever emotions they're experiencing, whether it's sadness, anger, guilt, or numbness. Avoid minimizing their feelings or trying to cheer them up with clichés.

* OFFER PRACTICAL SUPPORT: Help out with everyday tasks such as cooking, running errands, or housework. These small gestures can make a big difference and reduce their mental load.

* DON'T OVERWHELM THEM: Often, when someone dies, people flock to rally around their loved ones. While this comes from a place of love and kindness, having to be constantly ready to receive guests and manage the schedule of people wanting to visit to pay their respects may add unnecessary stress to the bereaved. Try to read the situation and let your loved one set the tone for how much alone time they want.

* RESPECT THEIR GRIEVING PROCESS: Understand that everyone grieves differently and at their own pace. Don't impose your own expectations or timeline for how they should feel or cope with their loss.

* AVOID CLICHÉS: While they might be well intentioned, phrases like "everything happens for a reason" or "they're in a better place now" can be perceived as hurtful and dismissive.

* ENCOURAGE SELF-CARE: Remind your loved one to take care of themselves, both physically and emotionally. Keeping up with simple self-care like sufficient sleep, basic skincare, and nutritious food is crucial for your mental and physical well-being when you're going through difficult times.

* OFFER ONGOING SUPPORT: Grieving doesn't end after the funeral or memorial service. Continue to check in with your loved one regularly and be particularly mindful to reach out on anniversaries, birthdays, and other significant dates related to the person's loss.

* POINT THEM TOWARD PROFESSIONAL HELP IF NEEDED: If you're concerned about your loved one's physical, mental, or emotional well-being, encourage them to seek support from a therapist, grief counselor, or support group.

Productive procrastination

Ahh, procrastination. We all do it. Staring blankly out the window, scrolling mindlessly on our phone, or pointlessly rearranging our sock drawer while trying not to make eye contact with that task on our to-do list with the looming deadline. But we're not here to get you to stop procrastinating (we're not that powerful)—we're here to tell you how to do it productively. Here's the trick: if you spend your procrastination time doing teeny-weeny but meaningful jobs, you'll give your brain the mini achievement boost it needs to get the ball rolling on the task you're actually supposed to be doing. Sounds too good to be true? Try it for yourself.

HOW TO HACK YOUR PROCRASTINATION TIME

- **CLEAN/DECLUTTER:** Don't get carried away and do the whole house, Mary Poppins—just tick one job off your list.

- **UNSUBSCRIBE FROM EMAILS/CLEAR YOUR INBOX:** As the ancient saying goes, a clear inbox equals a clear mind (pretty sure it was Plato who said that).

- **WATER YOUR PLANTS:** But only if they need it! Being a world-class procrastinator is not an excuse to drown your houseplants.

- **DO SOME EXERCISE:** This could be something quick (like a 60-second plank, some stretches, or a bit of chair yoga), a walk around the block, or do a full workout. Exercise has a whole load of positive mental health benefits and has been shown to improve productivity.

- **DO SOME MEAL PLANNING:** Get a headstart on your meal prep for the week by planning out your meals and ingredient list for your next shopping trip (you can also use this time to do a quick inventory to see what you've already got in the pantry, fridge, and freezer).

- **LEARN A LANGUAGE:** Jump on a language app for a quick, productive procrastination session that will light up different parts of your brain.

- **DO SOMETHING CREATIVE:** Just like learning a language, a quick burst of creativity will unlock different parts of your brain and might just give you the space and time you need to get into the zone to tackle the task at hand.

- **LEAVE ONLINE REVIEWS FOR LOCAL BUSINESSES:** As you learned when you were hanging out with the Community Crew, writing positive online reviews for businesses is a fantastic way to be a force for good in your local community.

- **CATCH UP ON YOUR MESSAGES:** If you've been a bit caught up in your busy adult life recently, take a few minutes to respond to those latest messages in the group chat or give your family a quick call to check in.

How to break up with your friends

Back on page 102 when you took a ride on the Relationship Rollercoaster, you learned how to let down someone you're dating kindly, but firmly. Rejection is never easy, but it can be even harder when it's a friend you want to break up with. Friendship breakups can be just as devastating as romantic breakups—if not more—and there's far less advice out there for how to go about it. We've pulled together some tips to help you navigate these choppy waters.

HOW TO KNOW WHEN IT'S TIME TO LET SOMEONE GO

- You no longer look forward to seeing them. You know the feeling—that sudden knot in the pit of your stomach when you find out a certain person will be at a party or on a group trip. Listen to your gut, it's time to let them go.

- You feel exhausted after spending time with them. Whether it's because they constantly complain, don't respect your boundaries, or just have a chaotic energy that drains your social battery, you deserve to be around people who lift you up, not bring you down.

- You don't trust them. If you suspect your friend is keeping things from you, being disrespectful about you, or breaking your trust, the relationship is already broken. Time to make it official.

HOW TO CUT THE CORD

- STEP BACK GRADUALLY: If you'd rather reduce or sever contact in an amicable, non-confrontational way, try gradually pulling away. Leave longer and longer gaps between replying to messages, make yourself increasingly unavailable for chats, and drop out of contact. While this isn't generally recommended for dating (you should always be upfront and let people know where they stand in a romantic relationship), in long-term friendships it's not always that straightforward, especially if you're part of a wider friendship group. Your friend may take the hint or the friendship may organically cool off. Who knows, once you've had a bit of space, you might find you see the friendship in a new light.

- TACKLE IT HEAD-ON: If gradually pulling away hasn't worked or you'd rather just tear off the bandage and get it over with, have an open, honest discussion with your friend. Explain why you're stepping back from the friendship with as much empathy, clarity, and maturity as possible. A good tip is to prepare for the conversation in advance, practice what you're going to say, and try to anticipate your friend's reaction so that you can have well-thought-out responses that get your message across clearly while minimizing any hurt feelings.

Sorry seems to be the hardest word

We've all said and done things we're not proud of and been left with that awful, gnawing, guilty feeling of knowing we made a bad call. Perhaps you said something you didn't mean in the heat of an argument, made an insensitive joke without thinking, or let someone down who trusted you. Whatever it is, an important part of being an adult is owning up to your mistakes and accepting responsibility for them with grace and sincerity.

HOW TO MAKE A SINCERE APOLOGY

- **STEP 1: TAKE OWNERSHIP.** As soon as you realize you've messed up, own up to it. Don't make excuses or shift the blame onto other people. Acknowledge your role in what happened and accept responsibility for your behavior.
- **STEP 2: APOLOGIZE SINCERELY AND MEAN IT.** Show remorse for your actions and the impact they had on the other person. Use language that conveys your genuine regret. If at any point in your apology you find yourself using the word "but," you've taken a wrong turn.
- **STEP 3: LISTEN.** Give the other person an opportunity to express how they feel and the impact your actions had on them. Don't interrupt or get defensive, just listen.
- **STEP 4: MAKE AMENDS.** If appropriate, offer to make it up to the other person. Ask them how you can make things right or take it upon yourself to set things straight (remember, you're responsible for what you did so you're responsible for making it right).
- **STEP 5: LEARN FROM YOUR MISTAKE.** Reflect on what led to you making the mistake in the first place and think about what you can do differently in the future to make sure it doesn't happen again. Learn from your mistake, forgive yourself, and move on.

WHAT'S A NON-APOLOGY?

A non-apology is a weak, blame-shifting excuse poorly disguised as an apology. They suggest that the problem is with the victim rather than with the person who made the mistake. Whatever you do, evict these from your vocabulary—they're a form of gaslighting, and you're better than that.

APOLOGY	NON-APOLOGY
"I'm sorry."	"I'm sorry if you feel that way."
"I'm sorry I offended you."	"I'm sorry if you were offended."
"I made a mistake."	"Mistakes were made."
"I'm sorry, I realize now that wasn't funny."	"It was only a joke, I'm sorry you didn't get it."
"I'm sorry, I overstepped."	"I was only trying to help."
"I'm sorry, I took it too far."	"You started it!"

That's a wrap!

Congratulations! You've now officially completed your access-all-areas tour of Adult Land! That's right, you're a fully-fledged adult now—well, maybe not fully fledged, but certainly capable of flying the nest on your own without immediately hitting the ground.

There was a lot to digest, so take this opportunity to give yourself a little breather and look back with a well-earned sense of pride on all the new knowledge you've picked up along the way.

Throughout this guide, you've learned invaluable lessons in navigating love and relationships, prioritizing your health and well-being, building a career you love, managing your finances, making technology work for you, maintaining a happy home, and being a valuable member of your community. You discovered how to take care of yourself inside and out, as well as how to cultivate meaningful relationships with those who will shape your journey through adulthood. You learned how to protect yourself financially, digitally, emotionally, and physically, and how to build a life that brings you ultimate fulfillment, peace, and happiness. Not bad for under 200 pages!

Armed with this newfound knowledge and confidence, you're now better equipped than ever to tackle the ups and downs of adulthood with grace, strength, and resilience (or, at the very least, make it seem like you know what you're doing—which, let's face it, is half the battle).

Of course, we don't expect you to have memorized everything on the first go, so be sure to keep this book somewhere handy so you can whip it out whenever you find yourself face-to-face with a new adult-y challenge. Fold down the pages, fill it with sticky notes, scribble in the margins, tattoo the steps for how to boil an egg onto your lower back—whatever works for you to keep all this info front of mind as you venture forth into this exciting new chapter in your life.

And remember—your journey is just beginning. There will be highs and lows, breakthroughs and setbacks, dinner party triumphs, and disastrous dates, but with each challenge comes an opportunity for growth and self-discovery. Try to embrace the lows as much as the highs, and look at every experience—good and bad—as a chance to level up your adult life skills.

Above all, remember that you're not alone. Whether you're turning to your friends, family, colleagues, housemates, mentors, or community for advice, know that we're all out here, cheering you on every step of the way. So, enjoy your time in Adult Land—we're so excited to have you!

Glossary

APPRAISAL
Evaluation of a property's value by a professional.

ASBESTOS
A heat-resistant, fibrous mineral used in building materials, now known to cause health issues.

BIAS
Prejudice or favoritism toward a particular thing, person, or group.

BOTS
Automated software applications that perform tasks online, often repetitive or malicious.

BURNOUT
Physical or mental exhaustion due to prolonged stress or overwork.

CONSULATE
The office of a foreign government that provides services to its citizens in another country.

CROWDFUNDING
Funding a project by raising small amounts of money from a large number of people, typically via the internet.

CV (RÉSUMÉ)
A document summarizing your education, work experience, skills, and achievements.

DEDUCTIBLES
The amount the policyholder must pay out-of-pocket before their insurance coverage begins.

DEEP FAKES
Synthetic media generated using AI, often to depict false events or speeches.

DEPOSIT
Money placed as security or partial payment toward a purchase or rental agreement.

DIVIDENDS
Payments made to shareholders from a company's profits.

DOPAMINE
A chemical messenger in the brain that's associated with pleasure and reward.

EMBASSY
The base for a diplomatic mission which represents one country in another.

ERGONOMIC
Designed for efficiency and comfort in the working environment.

ETIQUETTE
Accepted norms of behavior in social or professional settings.

FORECLOSURE
The legal process by which a lender repossesses a property due to non-payment of the mortgage.

GROUTING
The material used to fill gaps between tiles or bricks.

GUARANTOR
Someone who agrees to pay your rent or debt on your behalf if you can't.

HOARDING
The excessive accumulation of possessions, often to the detriment of your living space and/or health.

INVENTORY
A documented list of a property's contents and condition at the start of the tenancy.

LANDFILL
A site for disposing of waste materials by burying them.

LIABILITY
Legal responsibility for damages or losses.

LIMESCALE
A hard, chalky deposit often found in kettles, pipes, and appliances due to mineral build-up.

MINIMALISM
A lifestyle or design philosophy emphasising simplicity and lack of clutter.

MORTGAGE
A loan secured by property, typically used for purchasing real estate.

NICHE
A specialized segment of the market or area of interest.

ROYALTIES
Payments you get whenever someone buys or uses your intellectual property.

SABOTAGE
Deliberate action to undermine or disrupt something.

SENSATIONALISM
Presentation of information in a way that exaggerates or distorts reality to evoke strong reactions.

SOFT SKILLS
Non-technical skills related to communication, teamwork, and interpersonal abilities.

TROLL
Someone who posts inflammatory or off-topic messages online to provoke oth

UTILITIES
Services such as electricity, water, and gas.

WALLFLOWER
Someone who prefers to observe rather than participate in social situations.